JUNIOR DRUG AWARENESS

Vicodin, OxyContin, and Other Pain Relievers

JUNIOR DRUG AWARENESS

JUNIOR DRUG AWARENESS

Vicodin, OxyContin, and Other Pain Relievers

Amy E. Breguet

CHELSEA HOUSE
PUBLISHERS
An imprint of Infobase Publishing

Junior Drug Awareness: Vicodin, OxyContin, and Other Pain Relievers

Copyright © 2008 by Infobase Publishing

Chelsea House
An imprint of Infobase Publishing
132 West 31st Street
New York NY 10001

Library of Congress Cataloging-in-Publication Data

Breguet, Amy.
  Vicodin, OxyContin, and other pain relievers / Amy E. Breguet.
      p. cm. — (Junior drug awareness)
  Includes bibliographical references and index.
  ISBN 978-0-7910-9700-7 (hardcover)
  1. Narcotics. 2. Opioids. 3. Oxycodone. I. Title. II. Series.

  RM328.B74 2008
  362.29'3—dc22   2007032350

Chelsea House books are available at special discounts when purchased in bulk quantities for businesses, associations, institutions, or sales promotions. Please call our Special Sales Department in New York at (212) 967-8800 or (800) 322-8755.

You can find Chelsea House on the World Wide Web at http://www.chelseahouse.com

Text design by Erik Lindstrom
Cover design by Jooyoung An

Printed in the United States

Bang NMSG 10 9 8 7 6 5 4 3 2 1

This book is printed on acid-free paper.

All links and web addresses were checked and verified to be correct at the time of publication. Because of the dynamic nature of the web, some addresses and links may have changed since publication and may no longer be valid.

CONTENTS

Battling a Pandemic: A History of Drugs in the United States

When Johnny came marching home again after the Civil War, he probably wasn't marching in a very straight line. This is because Johnny, like 400,000 of his fellow drug-addled soldiers, was addicted to morphine. With the advent of morphine and the invention of the hypodermic needle, drug addiction became a prominent problem during the nineteenth century. It was the first time such widespread drug dependence was documented in history.

Things didn't get much better in the later decades of the nineteenth century. Cocaine and opiates were used as over-the-counter "medicines." Of course, the most famous was Coca-Cola, which actually did contain cocaine in its early days.

After the turn of the twentieth century, drug abuse was spiraling out of control, and the United States government stepped in with the first regulatory controls. In 1906, the Pure Food and Drug Act became a law. It required the labeling of product ingredients. Next came the Harrison Narcotics Tax Act of 1914, which outlawed illegal importation or distribution of cocaine and opiates. During this time, neither the medical community nor the general population was aware of the principles of addiction.

After the passage of the Harrison Act, drug addiction was not a major issue in the United States until the 1960s, when drug abuse became a much bigger social problem. During this time, the federal government's drug enforcement agencies were found to be ineffective. Organizations often worked against one another, causing counterproductive effects. By 1973, things had gotten so bad that President Richard Nixon, by executive order, created the Drug Enforcement Administration (DEA), which became the lead agency in all federal narcotics investigations. It continues in that role to this day. The effectiveness of enforcement and the so-called "Drug War" are open to debate. Cocaine use has been reduced by 75% since its peak in 1985. However, its replacement might be methamphetamine (speed, crank, crystal), which is arguably more dangerous and is now plaguing the country. Also, illicit drugs tend to be cyclical, with various drugs, such as LSD, appearing, disappearing, and then reappearing again. It is probably closest to the truth to say that a war on drugs can never be won, just managed.

Fighting drugs involves a three-pronged battle. Enforcement is one prong. Education and prevention is the second. Treatment is the third.

Although pandemics of drug abuse have been with us for more than 150 years, education and prevention were not seriously considered until the 1970s. In 1982, former First Lady Betty Ford made drug treatment socially acceptable with the opening of the Betty Ford Center. This followed her own battle with addiction. Other treatment centers—including Hazelton, Fair Oaks, and Smithers (now called the Addiction Institute of New York)—added to the growing number of clinics, and soon detox facilities were in almost every city. The cost of a single day in one of these facilities is often more than $1,000, and the effectiveness of treatment centers is often debated. To this day, there is little regulation over who can practice counseling.

It soon became apparent that the most effective way to deal with the drug problem was prevention by education. By some estimates, the overall cost of drug abuse to society exceeds $250 billion per year; preventive education is certainly the most cost-effective way to deal with the problem. Drug education can save people from misery, pain, and ultimately even jail time or death. In the early 1980s, First Lady Nancy Reagan started the "Just Say No" program. Although many scoffed at the program, its promotion of total abstinence from drugs has been effective with many adolescents. In the late 1980s, drug education was not science based, and people essentially were throwing mud at the wall to see what would stick. Motivations of all types spawned hundreds, if not thousands, of drug-education programs. Promoters of some programs used whatever political clout they could muster to get on various government agencies' lists of most effective programs. The bottom line, however, is that prevention is very difficult to quantify. It's nearly impossible to prove that drug use would have occurred if it were not prevented from happening.

In 1983, the Los Angeles Unified School District, in conjunction with the Los Angeles Police Department, started what was considered at that time to be the gold standard of school-based drug education programs. The program was called Drug Abuse Resistance Education, otherwise known as D.A.R.E. The program called for specially trained police officers to deliver drug-education programs in schools. This was an era in which community-oriented policing was all the rage. The logic was that kids would give street credibility to a police officer who spoke to them about drugs. The popularity of the program was unprecedented. It spread all across the country and around the world. Ultimately, 80% of American school districts would utilize the program. Parents, police officers, and kids all loved it. Unexpectedly, a special bond was formed between the kids who took the program and the police officers who ran it. Even in adulthood, many kids remember the name of their D.A.R.E. officer.

By 1991, national drug use had been halved. In any other medical-oriented field, this figure would be astonishing. The number of people in the United States using drugs went from about 25 million in the early 1980s to 11 million in 1991. All three prongs of the battle against drugs vied for government dollars, with each prong claiming credit for the reduction in drug use. There is no doubt that each contributed to the decline in drug use, but most people agreed that preventing drug abuse before it started had proved to be the most effective strategy. The National Institute on Drug Abuse (NIDA), which was established in 1974, defines its mandate in this way: "NIDA's mission is to lead the Nation in bringing the power of science to bear on drug abuse and addiction." NIDA leaders were the experts in prevention and treatment, and they had enormous resources. In

1986, the nonprofit Partnership for a Drug-Free America was founded. The organization defined its mission as, "Putting to use all major media outlets, including TV, radio, print advertisements and the Internet, along with the pro bono work of the country's best advertising agencies." The Partnership for a Drug-Free America is responsible for the popular campaign that compared "your brain on drugs" to fried eggs.

The American drug problem was front-page news for years up until 1990–1991. Then the Gulf War took over the news, and drugs never again regained the headlines. Most likely, this lack of media coverage has led to some peaks and valleys in the number of people using drugs, but there has not been a return to anything near the high percentage of use recorded in 1985. According to the University of Michigan's 2006 Monitoring the Future study, which measured adolescent drug use, there were 840,000 fewer American kids using drugs in 2006 than in 2001. This represents a 23% reduction in drug use. With the exception of prescription drugs, drug use continues to decline.

In 2000, the Robert Wood Johnson Foundation recognized that the D.A.R.E. Program, with its tens of thousands of trained police officers, had the top state-of-the-art delivery system of drug education in the world. The foundation dedicated $15 million to develop a cutting-edge prevention curriculum to be delivered by D.A.R.E. The new D.A.R.E. program incorporates the latest in prevention and education, including high-tech, interactive, and decision-model-based approaches. D.A.R.E. officers are trained as "coaches" who support kids as they practice research-based refusal strategies in high-stakes peer-pressure environments. Through stunning magnetic resonance imaging (MRI) images, students get to see tangible proof of how various substances diminish brain activity.

Will this program be the solution to the drug problem in the United States? By itself, probably not. It is simply an integral part of a larger equation that everyone involved hopes will prevent kids from ever starting to use drugs. The equation also requires guidance in the home, without which no program can be effective.

Ronald J. Brogan
Regional Director
D.A.R.E America

Pain, Pain, Go Away

No one is safe from feeling pain. Pains are those all-too-familiar sensations that—depending on their cause and other factors—may be described as throbbing, pounding, burning, searing, or stabbing, to cite just a few typical adjectives. Although everybody feels pain from time to time, more than a quarter of the U.S. population age 20 and older reports having experienced pain for a period of longer than 24 hours. That's more than 76 million Americans. Many of these people suffer from **chronic** pain, meaning they are in pain essentially all the time. For them, pain is more than an unpleasant experience. It's something that affects how they live every day.

THE MOST COMMON COMPLAINT

Pain is a part of countless diseases and medical conditions. It's no wonder that this general symptom is the number-one reason people see their doctors. Back pain, the kind most commonly reported, is the leading cause of disability in Americans under 45 years old. Other types of muscle and bone pain, such as pain in the neck, shoulder, hip, or knee, are also common. Headaches (including migraines) and jaw or facial pain are often reported, too. Pain is considered acute when it is caused by an injury, a temporary illness (such as an ear infection or flu), or a medical procedure. Chronic pain may result from an injury that did not heal properly or caused lasting damage. A disease, such as arthritis or cancer, can also cause chronic pain. In some cases, doctors cannot find any clear cause for a sufferer's chronic pain. For this reason, many medical experts consider chronic pain to be a disease in itself.

Physical discomfort, although the most obvious problem associated with chronic pain, is far from the only one. Many people with chronic pain sleep poorly several nights per week, which results in exhaustion that affects daily functioning. For some people, tasks as simple as opening a jar or climbing stairs might become dreaded chores, or even impossible. Pain sufferers may be forced to limit leisure activities, such as playing a sport or going out with friends. Situations like these often lead to emotional distress, including depression, anxiety, anger, loneliness, or feelings of hopelessness. According to a 2007 survey conducted by Partners Against Pain, one-third of chronic pain sufferers say "they would spend all of their money on pain treatment if they knew it would work."

Then there is the bigger picture. Disabling pain can mean missed workdays, weeks, or months, resulting in

income loss for the person and less productive companies. These losses, when added to health-care expenses
connected with pain, total an estimated $100 billion
dollars in the United States—for a single year.

OVER-THE-COUNTER RELIEF

Fortunately, some simple treatments do work for pain
sufferers. The first thing most people do to treat pain is
reach for the medicine cabinet, or run to the drugstore,
for a **nonprescription** pain reliever. Nonprescription
pain relievers are those that can be bought without
getting a doctor's permission. Frequently, pain sufferers choose a nonsteroidal anti-inflammatory drug, or
NSAID for short. NSAIDs work by interfering with the
creation of prostaglandins, which are **hormones** that
trigger pain. Aspirin was the original NSAID. It was first
introduced in Europe more than 100 years ago and is
still a popular treatment today.

Aspirin has many benefits. It can relieve mild or
moderate pain and inflammation (redness and swelling), reduce fever, and even help prevent a heart attack.
But it had its downsides, too. These include its nega-
tive effect on the digestive system, also known as the
gastrointestinal (GI) system. It also poses a special risk
for children and teenagers. When taken during a case of
flu or chicken pox, aspirin is linked with a rare but serious brain disease called Reye's Syndrome. Young people
should talk to their doctors before taking aspirin or any
other drug containing the ingredient *salicylate*, such
as Excedrin, Alka-Seltzer, Dristan, and Pepto-Bismol.
In general, people under age 18 should avoid these
medications.

Avoiding aspirin is likely not a problem for today's
teens, since another effective nonprescription NSAID—
ibuprofen—has been widely available since the 1980s. It

While the strongest pain relievers require a doctor's recommendation and written prescription, nonprescription medicines such as aspirin and ibuprofen are often used to treat minor aches and pains and fever. These over-the-counter drugs, as seen here lining the shelves of a drugstore, are not as strong as prescription drugs, but they can still be abused.

is better known as Advil, Motrin, and by its other **brand names**. Ibuprofen was introduced in the United States in the late 1970s and was approved for nonprescription, or "over the counter" (OTC), use in 1984. Today it is one of the most commonly used drugs in the country. For the general population, ibuprofen may have a few benefits over aspirin. These mainly relate to the ways NSAIDs can affect the GI system. Although all NSAIDs carry some risk of causing stomach and other GI problems, such as bleeding or ulcers, studies show that these risks are lowest with ibuprofen. Since the degree of risk is largely connected to how much of the drug is taken and for how long, the key is to always take it exactly as directed on the package unless otherwise advised by a health-care provider.

The second major type of nonprescription pain reliever is acetaminophen, otherwise known by the brand name Tylenol. Acetaminophen reduces fever by affecting the "heat center" of the brain. It also raises a person's ability to tolerate pain, therefore relieving it. (Tylenol's effects on inflammation are unclear.) It generally doesn't cause the GI problems that NSAIDs can, making it a good choice for people who can't tolerate NSAIDs well for that reason. Acetaminophen is also often the first choice for relieving children's pain. It is not without its risks, though. The primary risk associated with acetaminophen use is liver poisoning, although this is an uncommon occurrence. Still, it is extremely important to follow the instructions on the medicine package exactly, and to pay attention to warnings about how the drug behaves when mixed with alcohol and other drugs.

Although acetaminophen and common NSAIDs are available in any drugstore, these drugs are sometimes combined with other, stronger medications called **opioids**. The resulting combination drug is now considered an opioid, too, and it requires a **prescription**.

OPIOIDS: THE NEXT LINE OF DEFENSE

Sometimes, nonprescription pain relievers are not enough. For example, surgery or a serious injury can result in greater pain than a couple of aspirin tablets can

Poppies are a source of heroin, opium, and several popular pain medications. Many of the plants are illegally grown in Afghanistan. In 2007, the opium and heroin made from Afghan poppies were estimated to be worth about one-third of the national economy of Afghanistan. Here, an Afghan farmer inspects his poppy crop for harvest. The gum that bleeds out of the plant when it's slightly cut is raw opium.

handle. This might also be the case for many types of chronic pain, especially severe arthritis, back pain caused by spinal problems, and pain associated with some types of cancer or autoimmune diseases (disorders in which the body "fights" itself). When NSAIDs or acetaminophen alone cannot treat pain, a doctor might prescribe a medication belonging to a class called opiates, or opioids.

Opiates, as the name suggests, are drugs that come from the opium poppy plant. Opium was in use for thousands of years, at first for its calming and mood-lifting effects, before it was recognized as a valuable medicine. The Bayer company first introduced the opioid heroin as a cough medicine ingredient in 1898, and the drug was still used medically until 1970. Now, however, heroin is associated only with **recreational** use and **addiction**. On the other hand, the opioid morphine, introduced to medicine nearly a century before heroin, has stood the test of time.

Through the years, several new painkillers have been developed that are either part-opiate or chemically designed to work like opiates. Today there are dozens of such medications—known as opioids—on the market. All of them require a prescription, and some are mainly administered by health-care professionals. (In this text, *opioids* will refer to both natural opiates and **synthetic** opioids unless otherwise noted.) Morphine and other **narcotics** relieve pain by blocking pain signals sent to the spinal cord and brain. More powerful than nonprescription drugs, morphine and drugs made from it can prevent a person from feeling even the most traumatic and severe kinds of pain.

Of course, something this strong has its drawbacks. The first concern a doctor might have when prescribing an opioid is possible side effects. These vary among particular drugs. Most drugs carry some risk of nausea or vomiting, itching, constipation, drowsiness, or dizziness. Some of these side effects may wear off after the person's body adjusts to the drug. If the effects don't wear off, or if they are bothersome, a doctor may decide to switch the patient to one of the many other opioids available. Not only do side effects vary depending on the drug, but a particular drug's effects can also differ from person to person.

The other, and more serious, concern regarding opioids is their potential for addiction and abuse. As noted

(continues on page 22)

AS OLD AS PAIN ITSELF:
AN OPIUM TIMELINE

Evidence of opium use dates back more than 5,000 years. Here's a glimpse of its evolution:

3400 B.C.* Ancient Sumerians, who lived in what is today southeastern Iraq, grow and use the poppy plant, which they call *hul gil*—"the plant of joy."

1300 B.C. Opium use spreads to Greece, Rome, and Arab countries. Doctors in these regions describe in ancient medical texts its poisonous potential.

460 B.C. Hippocrates, a famous doctor from ancient Greece who is today known as the "father of medicine," uses

Hippocrates, a doctor from ancient Greece known by many as the "father of medicine," dismissed claims that opium had magical properties. Yet, he also recognized opium's use in treating internal diseases and epidemics.

(continues on page 20)

(continued from page 19)

opium to treat pain. He also uses the drug to treat a variety of other sicknesses, including coughs and "diseases of women."

A.D. 1300s–1500 Opium disappears from historical records during the Inquisition, a movement by the Catholic Church to, in part, end many practices considered satanic. Non-European customs—including opium use—fall into this category.

1527 The Swiss scientist Paracelsus reintroduces opium in Europe during the height of the Protestant religious movement known as Reformation. He describes "Stones of Immortality," black pills made from opium and other ingredients that are given as painkillers. Around this time, some evidence of **tolerance** and **physical dependence** arises.

1680 Doctors throughout Europe turn back to opium for various medical purposes, following a period when many people think of the substance as an old-fashioned and dangerous kind of medicine. English doctor Thomas Sydenham writes, "So necessary an instrument is opium in the hand of a skillful man, that medicine would be a cripple without it."

1805 In Germany, a pharmacist's assistant named Friedrich Wilhelm Serturner removes the ingredient in opium that is responsible for the plant's effects on people. He studies the substance and calls the purified white powder *morphium*, which is soon known as morphine. Doctors say it is "God's own medicine."

1827 The German medicine company E. Merck & Company begins to produce morphine in large amounts.

1874 English researcher C.R. Wright boils morphine over a stove, creating heroin.

Early 1900s Believing that heroin is not addictive, many physicians recommend it as a way to help morphine addicts step down gradually. This thinking is proven terribly wrong when heroin addiction becomes an even bigger problem than morphine addiction.

1924 The U.S. government bans nonmedical use of opioids.

1970 The United States's Federal Controlled Substance Act bans heroin altogether, declaring that it has no accepted medical use.

1984 The U.S. Food and Drug Administration (FDA) approves the use of Vicodin.

1995 The FDA approves the use of OxyContin.

2003 The number of Americans dependent on opioids reaches about 2 million.

*years given are approximate

(continued from page 18)
earlier, the people who discovered opiates thousands of years ago weren't using them only for their pain-relieving properties. They found that these substances could relax them and produce other pleasurable effects. Several thousand years later, it's well known that using any drug for this purpose is abuse, which in turn can lead to addiction. An addiction is a physical and psychological need for the drug. And when a drug is in control, a life is in serious trouble.

A MATTER OF BALANCE

Millions of people depend on opioids for valid medical reasons. Ironically, the doctor's prescription and accessibility of these drugs has made them easy to misuse. Some people might get their hands on opioids illegally—in some cases, without even realizing they're breaking the

 NEW DRUGS ON THE BLOCK

The opioids Vicodin and OxyContin are taking their place among the old pain medications, and have recently been added to the National Institute on Drug Abuse's Monitoring the Future (MTF) survey. The survey shows drug abuse trends among youth during three-year periods. Note that in the most recent survey—only the second survey to ask about the two painkillers—the usage rate in the past year for Vicodin alone exceeds the usage rates recorded for cocaine, LSD, meth, steroids, Ecstasy, and several other drugs.

law. Others may be prescribed a drug for genuine pain, but later end up crossing the line into recreational use. This scenario is often the start of addiction.

An ongoing goal among health-care professionals who deal with pain—and government agencies that deal with drug policy—is keeping up the delicate balance between helping and hurting. Although experts agree that opioids are a valuable tool for pain management, controversy often surrounds the management of the drugs themselves. The patient and his or her doctor, as well as government drug agencies, must work together to crack the problems of abuse and addiction.

Health-care providers must listen carefully to a patient who has pain. They need to make informed decisions on what type of medication to prescribe, based on the patient's medical problem, age, and medical and family history. Doctors must also take into account the specific ways that the pain affects the patient's daily life, and many other factors, too. Health-care providers also need to closely monitor the patient's progress, pain reduction, and side effects—starting as soon as the patient begins taking a drug. For their part, policymakers are constantly keeping track of trends in drug misuse and prescribing practices, as well as advances in drug science. Programs and systems designed to help discourage the abuse of painkillers are already in place.

The most important responsibility, some might argue, belongs to each individual. Understanding the benefits and dangers of prescription painkillers, including laws that involve them, can help people make wise choices about these drugs.

2

Opioids: Medical Uses Today

As scientific interest and research into the myster-
ies of pain have increased, countless new methods
for effective pain management have emerged. Many of
them have nothing to do with drugs. Yet, despite these
new and arguably safer treatments, there are still situations when doctors will call on opioids to help relieve a
patient's pain. In some cases, the benefits of these drugs
may even be considered the best choice.

PLANNED PAIN: OPIOIDS AFTER SURGERY

Pain associated with surgery can be severe. Fortunately,
because the "injuries" of an operation are carefully
planned, pain management can be, too. In fact, relief
typically starts even before the surgery does, when
patients are given one or more forms of anesthesia. This

PAIN RELIEF: COULD THE BEST MEDICATION BE NO MEDICATION?

Although many patients swear by the pain relief they experience from medications, a fast-growing number of other people are exploring pill-free routes to relief. And they are finding satisfying results. Below are just a few examples of some commonly used pain relief methods. Modern or age-old, these techniques have become important parts of millions of patients' pain management plans.

Acupuncture: Acupuncture is rooted in ancient Chinese medicine. It involves the insertion of thin needles into certain points on the body. These points are believed to be connected with particular internal organs or body systems. Inserting needles into these points is said to provide relief from various types of pain, as well as from countless other symptoms.

Chiropractic treatments: This refers to the practice of adjusting and massaging the spine to relieve back pain. The treatment is performed by health-care professionals called chiropractors. Many people seek chiropractic services for back or neck pain, but this type of treatment is also used for other physical problems.

Guided imagery: This is one of several mind-based therapies that have helped people with pain or emotional stress. The person imagines a process taking place and follows that process from beginning to end. For example, a patient experiencing pain might picture an object representing the pain, and "watch" the object getting smaller and smaller. Related techniques include visualization, meditation, and hypnosis.

Massage: This is the manipulation of muscles and soft tissues, usually practiced by a professional massage

(continues on page 26)

(continued from page 25)

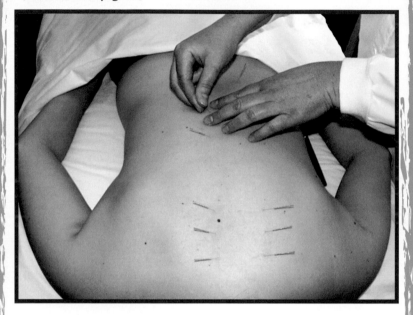

As an alternative to prescription medicine for pain relief, many people have turned to an ancient medical procedure, called acupuncture, in which thin needles are placed in certain points of the body. While research has shown how it can ease nausea and pain, only trained professionals should perform acupuncture.

therapist. Massage can work out muscle tightness and reduce the buildup of lactic acid, a substance believed to cause soreness in overused muscles.

Physical therapy: With the help of a professional physical therapist, a patient exercises particular muscle groups to achieve a health-related goal. This might be pain relief, an increase in physical abilities, rehabilitation after injury, or all of these.

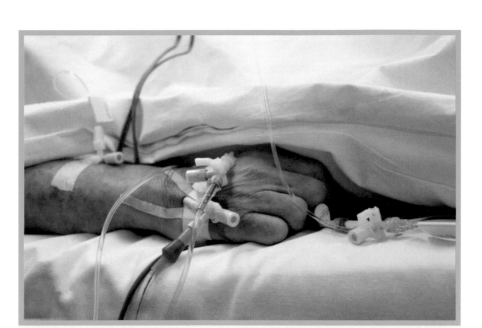

Anesthesia is usually injected into the body through a single injection, or in a continuous stream through intravenous (IV) therapy. Here, a patient's hand is seen with an intravenous hookup, commonly used to administer painkillers before surgery.

refers to drugs that reduce or take away physical feelings. General anesthesia makes a patient unconscious for surgery, while local or regional anesthesia just numbs the body part or parts the surgery will affect. These are usually given as a single injection or through a needle called an **IV** (short for the word *intravenous*, or "in veins") that continuously drips the anesthesia into the patient's bloodstream.

Because patients already have anesthesia going into surgery, some of the edge is taken off the pain they would otherwise feel afterwards. Still, pain-relieving drugs—including opioids—are often a part of the plan for after an operation. In fact, opioids are sometimes mixed with anesthetic drugs from the start. Following surgery, many patients are able to take advantage of a recent advance known as "patient-controlled analgesia," or PCA. With PCA, the patient is connected to a machine containing a supply of a strong drug such as morphine. If the patient's pain increases, he or she can release a controlled amount of the drug into his body with the push of a button. This isn't as dangerous as it may sound. The system has strict controls in place that limit the amount of drug that can be released and how often it can be released. Many health-care professionals see PCA as a major breakthrough in pain management in hospitals.

Many surgical patients may be sent home with a prescription for painkillers to take as needed. This typically includes those who have had a minor procedure, such as oral surgery, that doesn't require an overnight stay in the hospital. The health-care provider writing the prescription and the patient must work together to manage certain responsibilities.

Even in a hospital, the convenience and effectiveness of certain strong drugs may not outweigh the risk of side effects—or worse. For example, morphine and other strong drugs carry a high risk of nausea and vomiting, which many patients may not be able to tolerate. An even bigger worry is the ability of these drugs to slow breathing. Although dosages can be carefully watched, it may be difficult to know at first what's safe for each individual. In fact, one study showed that some doctors and nurses are so concerned about breathing problems that they prescribe or give out only a fraction of the drug amount that would be considered safe. So, patients may be taking these drugs, and yet still not be getting the relief they need.

To avoid these problems, some surgeons today are moving away from using opioids at all. Instead, they are trying to treat pain with a combination of local anesthesia and NSAIDs. This non-narcotic route does not have the side effects and dosage concerns associated with opioids. It also has been shown to help some patients have a more comfortable recovery. Still, for those surgical patients who are able to tolerate them, opioids are sometimes a pain remedy that can't be matched by any other.

TRAUMA: OPIOIDS IN THE ER

Unlike the pain of recovering from surgery, some of the severest pain is very much *un*planned. It can strike with no warning at all. A car accident, serious fall, workplace mishap, or other traumatic event might result in broken bones, damaged organs or tissues, injury to the brain or spinal cord, or severe burns. For pain like this, opioids often come into play.

Pain relief after traumatic injury can be tricky. For one thing, there may be additional risks to consider when giving drugs to someone who is severely injured. For example, doctors and nurses in a hospital must be careful when treating a newly arrived accident victim. Giving that person certain drugs could be deadly if he or she had been drinking alcohol or using other drugs when the injury happened. Also, narcotics can possibly make things worse for someone with a head injury or breathing problems. For these reasons, hospital workers need to examine the situation extremely carefully before starting an accident victim on a painkiller. And they must monitor him or her very closely.

For patients with spinal cord injuries, pain treatment may be further complicated by a condition known as central pain syndrome. This results from damage to nerves that control physical feelings. The condition causes intense burning, tingling, or uncomfortable feelings of hot or cold from even just a touch to the skin.

Opioids have limited or no effect on this kind of discomfort. Patients with central pain syndrome may be put on a combination of various other types of drugs—such as antidepressants and anticonvulsants—and may never be completely pain-free.

FOR CANCER PATIENTS, SOME COMFORT

A lot of pain management research focuses directly on one widespread family of diseases: cancer. That's because many types of cancer cause moderate to severe pain. Fortunately, this pain usually can be controlled or even eliminated. Opioid drugs are often part of that relief, particularly in late stages of the disease.

Opioids aren't usually the first line of defense against pain. Cancer pain is no exception. For mild cancer pain, doctors might begin with NSAIDs or drugs not officially used for pain relief. For example, anti-nausea or anti-anxiety drugs might help the patient feel more comfortable. If pain worsens, a doctor may add weaker narcotics, such as hydrocodone (Vicodin), codeine, or darvocet. Finally, if pain becomes severe, a doctor may switch the patient to morphine or another strong narcotic. Patients may be given morphine in pill form, as an injection, as a fluid to swallow, or through an IV.

When it comes to cancer, most experts share the philosophy that physical comfort is a priority. So, although they proceed with caution, doctors will usually approve or encourage whatever dose is required to safely relieve a patient's pain. It is extremely rare to become addicted to an opioid during cancer pain treatment. If side effects occur, they are usually not severe enough to make the patient want to stop taking the drug. For most patients with advanced cancer, the benefits of opioid treatment outweigh the risks.

THE CASE FOR CHRONIC PAIN

Surgery, severe accidents, and cancer are situations for which opioids are almost always an option. But what about the millions of people who are neither traumatically injured nor seriously ill, and yet live with pain day in and day out? For them, opioids may seem to be the last hope for a productive life.

Chronic pain can result from many conditions, or it can be an unexplained condition in itself. Some known causes and types of chronic pain include arthritis, chronic back or neck pain, and migraine headaches. Another common cause is fibromyalgia, a condition causing constant muscle aches and other discomfort.

In general, doctors prescribe opioids to these patients only after nonaddictive drugs and/or nondrug therapies have failed to provide the needed pain relief. For example, most patients have tried NSAIDs or acetaminophen many times by the time they or their doctors start talking about narcotics. They also may have tried (or are still taking) other drugs that are not general pain relievers. Those drugs might instead be meant to treat a specific condition—for example, an arthritis or migraine medication. Patients with low back pain or joint pain may get relief from occasional injections of corticosteroids (which reduce swelling) directly into the painful area. The benefit may only be temporary, however, and side effects are sometimes reported.

Once doctor and patient agree that a narcotic may be the best chance for pain relief, the next step is to start an open, honest, and complete discussion about what to do. The doctor will want to know about the patient's health and personal history, as well as the ways that pain affects the patient's life. The patient will need

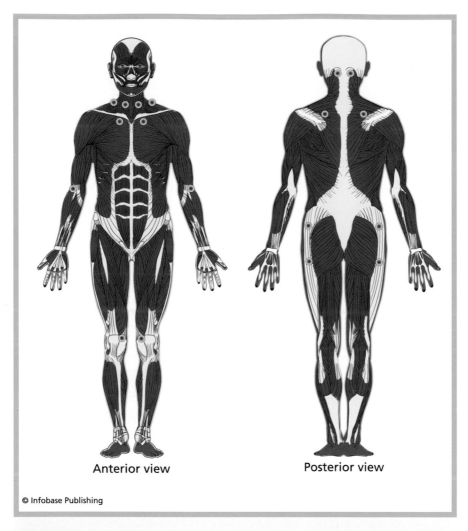

Anterior view   Posterior view

© Infobase Publishing

Even when over-the-counter medications fail to ease chronic pain, physicians are reluctant to prescribe narcotics to patients because of their addictive qualities. Patients who suffer from chronic diseases such as fibromyalgia, for instance, suffer from constant muscle, joint, and bone pain in specific areas, as pinpointed by circles in this diagram.

to know about the risks and benefits of any drug being considered. Together, the doctor and patient can make an informed decision on what drug to prescribe and at what dose. In general, they will start with the lowest effective dose possible.

In some cases, a doctor may prescribe more than one opioid. For example, a patient may benefit from an **extended-release** formula to be taken on a regular basis, as well as an **immediate-release** drug to take as needed during bad bouts of pain. Most opioids taken at home are pills, although a drug patch—which is applied to the skin and releases the drug continually—is available for severe pain. (This is rarely prescribed unless other opioids have been ineffective.) Once an opioid prescription has been given, the doctor's and patient's responsibilities have only just begun.

NOT TO BE TAKEN LIGHTLY: RESPONSIBLE USE OF AN OPIOID

When the doctor prescribes an opioid and the patient accepts it, the two have entered into a contract of sorts. The doctor has a responsibility to instruct the patient on exactly how and when to take the drug, and to provide him or her with all safety information. The doctor also has agreed to closely monitor the patient's use of the drug. This should involve:

- having the patient schedule monthly follow-up appointments (more frequent at first)
- asking the patient about his or her pain, any side effects, and quality of life at each appointment
- asking the patient how often he or she has needed to use immediate-release medication, if one was prescribed along with an extended-release formula
- adjusting dosages as needed

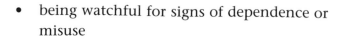

- being watchful for signs of dependence or misuse

Of course, the doctor must rely largely on what the patient tells him or her. Therefore, much of the responsibility for managing the drug falls on the patient. For his or her own safety—and maybe the safety of others—any patient who has been prescribed a narcotic should follow some basic rules:

1. Take the medication exactly as prescribed. Never make a change without discussing it with the doctor first. (This includes taking too little—don't be afraid to take the amount prescribed. If the patient isn't taking what was agreed upon, he or she will not get the full benefit of the drug and may complicate the pain management plan.)
2. Keep the medication in a safe place. Never give any of it—even a single pill—to someone else.
3. Keep all follow-up appointments. Answer the doctor's questions honestly, and report any concerns or side effects experienced.
4. Don't start taking any new medications, including herbal supplements, without talking to the doctor.
5. Be alert for signs of physical dependence or addiction. It is important that a patient is honest with his doctor—and him or herself—if he thinks he may have a problem.

Some doctors may even have patients sign an actual contract outlining each of their responsibilities,

THE DOCTOR-PATIENT AGREEMENT

To help ensure the safety and success of opioid treatment, a doctor and patient might sign a contract outlining their understanding of the treatment. By signing it, the patient agrees that he or she:

- will manage the prescription and the actual drug responsibly
- will store the drug safely and never give it to anyone else
- will not accept a controlled substance from another doctor without consulting the first doctor
- will contact the doctor with any questions or problems concerning the prescription
- may be subject to drug testing to make sure he or she is taking the medication as prescribed and is not taking any unauthorized drugs
- may have the prescription canceled for failure to follow the agreement

especially if the drug use is expected to be long-term. This can be a good way to help ensure safe and effective treatment.

3

Vicodin

"... I got addicted to that little pill. The reason I don't talk about it too much in the press is because it isn't funny, and I love to be funny in interviews. If you joke about that period in your life, it doesn't seem right."

—Actor Matthew Perry, of the TV show
Friends on his Vicodin addiction

Celebrity admissions. Illegal online sales. Theft and deceit. You've probably heard about the opioid drug best known as Vicodin. Like other prescription narcotics, Vicodin has an accepted medical use as a treatment for pain. It's also the most abused prescription painkiller in existence today.

A LEGITIMATE MEDICATION

Unlike the other pain-relieving drugs, Vicodin is actually a combination of two substances—an opioid and a nonopioid. Vicodin is part acetaminophen and part hydrocodone, the narcotic ingredient that puts this drug in the opioid category. Hydrocodone is also an anticough medicine and is found in some prescription cough syrups, although it's most frequently advertised as a painkiller. Hydrocodone also exists in combination with aspirin, ibuprofen, and allergy medications. But its most common partner, by far, is acetaminophen. Vicodin and other hydrocodone-based medications are the most frequently prescribed opioids in the United States. Vicodin and its **generic** versions make up 80% of hydrocodone prescriptions.

Vicodin is considered a weak opioid in terms of its chemical strength, and is prescribed for moderate to moderately severe pain. For example, it might be prescribed for use for a few days following a major dental procedure. Some people with chronic pain—from an injury or physical condition, or as a disorder in itself—may be prescribed Vicodin after other pain relief measures have proven insufficient. Vicodin comes in tablets, capsules, and liquid. Its most recognizable form is an oblong-shaped white tablet with a groove down the center. Each pill may be stamped with *VICODIN* or *V* (if it's the brand-name version), or the word *WATSON*, a capital *M*, or a capital *A* followed by a three-digit number.

Because it is made from an opioid and nonopioid, and because of its weakness compared to other opioid medications, Vicodin is a Schedule III drug. This means it is less strictly controlled than morphine, OxyContin, codeine, and most other narcotics. For example, a doctor may prescribe up to six months' worth of Vicodin, allowing the patient to get an initial 30-day supply of the drug and five **refills**. With Schedule II narcotics, a patient cannot get refills without getting a new prescription

 ## CLUB MED: VICODIN

Celebrities aren't necessarily the main users of prescription painkillers, but they're certainly the most hyped. These celebrities have learned about Vicodin's dangers the hard way—through recreational use of the drug:

- Former *Friends* TV star Matthew Perry twice spent time in rehab for an addiction to Vicodin and alcohol. The Vicodin addiction, Perry told interviewer Larry King, started as an effort to curb excessive alcohol use. He finally realized that he was in over his head. "I called a treatment center," Perry said. "I was smart enough even then to know that I couldn't possibly do this on my own."

- *The Simple Life* reality TV star Nicole Richie was pulled over for driving the wrong way on a freeway in December 2006. Richie admitted to police officers that she had smoked marijuana and taken Vicodin. She failed a test for alcohol and was arrested.

- Rapper Eminem has not only used Vicodin, he has also rapped about it. In addition to having

from a doctor. It's also legal to have Vicodin prescriptions from more than one doctor at once, which isn't legal with a Schedule II drug. Vicodin's Schedule III status may be, in part, what has sent it spiraling out of control.

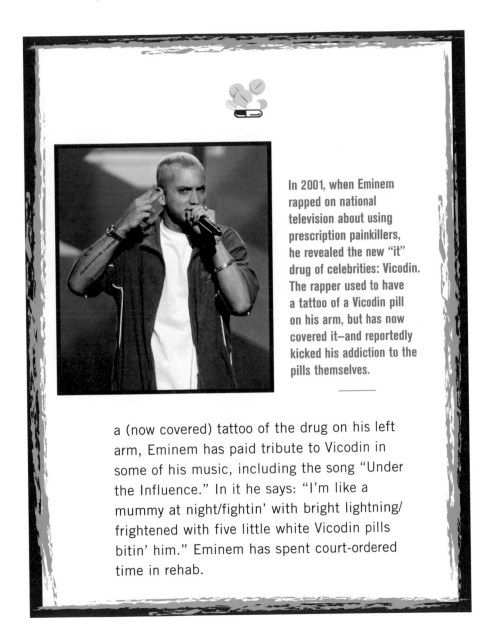

In 2001, when Eminem rapped on national television about using prescription painkillers, he revealed the new "it" drug of celebrities: Vicodin. The rapper used to have a tattoo of a Vicodin pill on his arm, but has now covered it—and reportedly kicked his addiction to the pills themselves.

a (now covered) tattoo of the drug on his left arm, Eminem has paid tribute to Vicodin in some of his music, including the song "Under the Influence." In it he says: "I'm like a mummy at night/fightin' with bright lightning/frightened with five little white Vicodin pills bitin' him." Eminem has spent court-ordered time in rehab.

DANGER BY CATEGORY: THE FEDERAL DRUG SCHEDULE

Under the Comprehensive Drug Abuse Prevention and Control Act of 1970, all drugs of potential abuse—including all narcotics—are considered "controlled substances." This means the government regulates their manufacture, importation, possession, and distribution. Each controlled substance falls into one of five "schedules," or categories, based on its potential for abuse, accepted medical use, and potential for addiction. Schedule I drugs are the most strictly controlled, and Schedule V are the least. Most prescription opioids are Schedule II because of their potential to be highly addictive. A notable exception is Vicodin, which is a Schedule III drug even though it is the most abused prescription painkiller in existence. Since all prescription opioids have some accepted medical use, none of them are Schedule I.

A DRUG OF UNMATCHED ABUSE

"At my high school, it is easier to get Vicodin than Children's Tylenol," wrote student Meena Hartenstein in a commentary for *Youth Radio*, a National Public Radio program. "Getting the school nurse to help you get rid of a headache requires signing a waiver and calling your parents. Most teens don't want to bother with that, so they grab a few painkillers from friends."

According to a 2006 study by the Office of National Drug Control Policy, more than half of teens say prescription pain relievers are "available everywhere." Nearly half of those who have used prescription pain relievers for "fun" said they got them for free from a friend or relative. More than 60% of teens say they can get them easily from their parents' medicine cabinets. With the light set of restrictions placed on Vicodin, it would make sense that this particular drug is often the one in question. In fact, the same study showed that, among twelfth graders, Vicodin was second only to marijuana in its frequency of use in the past year.

The words *Vicodin* and *hydrocodone* pop up more frequently than nearly any other painkiller in reports of *drug diversion*; that means any use of a drug other than its prescribed use. This includes use by someone other than the patient. Many times, however, mere "use" is the least of it. The following stories offer some disturbing examples.

September 2006: In Jacksonville, Florida, 12 young adults were arrested in connection with a prescription fraud ring known as "Operation Spinal Tab." One of the suspects' girlfriends was an employee at a spine health center. Using a copied set of keys, some of the suspects had broken into the center and stolen a prescription pad. They then proceeded to get more than 200 forged Lortab prescriptions filled at several Walgreens and CVS stores before getting busted.

March 2007: After an investigation by the Boone (North Carolina) Police Department and the Watauga County Sheriff's Office Narcotics Unit, three people were charged with several crimes related to running a "business" selling hydrocodone out of a private home. It was discovered that a one-year-old child was there during many of the drug sales. The baby was placed with the Department of Social Services.

January 2003: Drug regulators at the Nevada State Board of Pharmacy noticed that a small Internet pharmacy had filled more than 1,000 prescriptions for painkillers and other controlled substances in one month. An

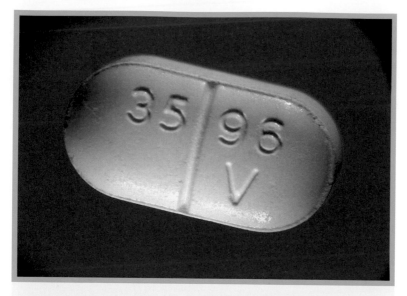

Vicodin pills are visually distinctive—white and oval, with a groove in the middle and the word *VICODIN* or the letter *V* stamped on the pill itself.

investigation revealed that the pharmacy had shipped more than 5 million doses of highly addictive drugs— including a full 10% of all hydrocodone prescribed in Nevada—to customers throughout the country. A 23-year-old woman—with help from her father, a convicted felon—was behind the electronic drug-trafficking enterprise. The Las Vegas–based Web site was quickly shut down.

March 2005: A 39-year-old resident of an assisted living facility in Dunedin, Florida, was arrested for the murder of a 22-year-old resident. The accused man, who had a prescription for hydrocodone, admitted to giving the victim 19 pills and sexually assaulting her. She died hours after the attack.

As these true stories make clear, Vicodin abuse can mean far more than taking a pill that belongs to someone else. Some experts attribute Vicodin's sudden rise in popularity (among both doctors and abusers) in recent years to a decline in the use of the Schedule II pain-killer OxyContin. That decline happened as reports of addictions, deaths, and lawsuits related to OxyContin

 ## BE WARY OF ONLINE MEDS

Since the beginning of the Internet, life has become a lot more convenient. For one thing, shopping has become something people can do without leaving their chairs. From one comfortable spot, consumers can buy nearly anything, from music to furniture to clothing—and even drugs.

In recent years, online pharmacies have popped up all over cyberspace. Many, such as those operated as part of honest stores' Web sites, are legitimate. Prescriptions are entered electronically, and then verified through a phar-macist's call to the prescribing doctor. Paper prescriptions can also be mailed. The problem, however, is that anyone can create and run a Web site. For that matter, anyone can create a Web site and call it a pharmacy. As a result, there are a lot of phony drugstores out there, set up largely to cash in on the prescription painkiller boom. Generic ver-sions of Vicodin are among these online crooks' biggest sellers.

Buying drugs from a shady online source can lead to trouble. The buyer might end up with stolen drugs or fake drugs. Or, the buyer might end up with no drugs at all—and possibly a letter from law enforcement—if police seized the drugs before they were successfully shipped. Unless an online pharmacy is clearly part of a real chain store, be wary, especially if the site claims that no prescrip-tion is needed (a sure sign of a bogus operation).

saturated the media. In light of the serious ways people have taken advantage of the availability of Vicodin and similar products, these drugs are currently under review for possible reclassification into Schedule II.

CAUTION: HYDROCODONE

In 1999, H. Guy Snyder had a successful career as CEO of the family-owned fast-food chain In-N-Out. His health, however, was another story. He suffered from hepatitis B and hepatitis C, and survived a heart attack in the mid-1990s. Then Snyder died at his California home at age 48. Sadly, it was neither the liver diseases nor heart problems that killed him. According to the medical report, the cause was much simpler: too much Vicodin. Snyder had a history of drug problems. In fact, both his hepatitis C and heart attack were drug-related, and he had overdosed before. His tragic story highlights the two biggest dangers attached to Vicodin and all prescription painkillers: addiction and death.

Some people seem to think that *legal* and *regulated* mean "safe." As many people have learned the hard way, this false belief can be dangerous—or flat-out deadly. In addition to the major consequences, there are many less serious but important risks that come with Vicodin use. This is true even for people who are taking the drug legally. The most basic of these is the possibility of side effects, most of which are harmless compared to the effects of other drugs. For example, someone taking Vicodin or a similar product may experience dizziness or lightheadedness, drowsiness, nausea, vomiting, stomach pain, constipation, difficulty urinating, and/or a rash. These symptoms may be mild and go away on their own. If they are bothersome, however, the patient should talk to his or her doctor about possibly switching to another medication. (And a patient who is drowsy

Steve Dotson, seen here in 2007, visits the bridge he used to live under when he was addicted to the prescription painkiller hydrocodone. His addiction caused intense cravings for the drug, and at one point, Dotson allowed his wife to drive over his leg so he could get more pills for the injury. He lost his job, his home, and custody of his children before giving up hydrocodone.

or dizzy should not drive a car until the symptoms resolve.)

Other possible effects may be signs of dangerous reactions to the drug. In the case of Vicodin, the symptom of greatest concern is breathing difficulty. Any patient who experiences breathing problems while taking Vicodin should call his or her doctor immediately.

Other risks to consider include drug allergies, as well as the possibility that Vicodin will interact dangerously with another medication being taken. Certain physical conditions may also make Vicodin use dangerous. Before accepting a prescription for Vicodin or any other opioid, patients should tell their doctors if they:

- know they are allergic to an ingredient in the drug, or to any medication
- are taking any other medications, especially other pain relievers, antidepressants, cough or cold medicines, or sleeping pills
- have a history of alcohol or other drug abuse

 HOUSE OF PAIN

Since the stuff of prime-time drama tends to mirror the real world, it's no wonder that Vicodin has made its way into TV storylines. Fans of FOX's medical TV hit *House*, along with the show's cast of characters, have become used to fact that title character Dr. Gregory House (British actor Hugh Laurie) couldn't get through an episode without popping a few white pills. Since choosing leg surgery over amputation years earlier, House had leaned as heavily on Vicodin as he had on his signature wooden cane. He obtained these pills mostly through physician friends and his own forged prescriptions.

The myth of the invincible doctor, however, came crashing down during the 2006 to 2007 season. House had problems with one of his patients, and that patient happened to be prickly, no-nonsense detective Michael Tritter (David Morse). Following an arrest (which was legal, although questionable), an intrusive investigation, a quick

- have (or have had) lung, liver, kidney, or thyroid disease, or urinary problems
- are pregnant or breastfeeding, or plan to become pregnant

Even taking Vicodin correctly and responsibly requires some caution. Yet, taking too much of any opioid can cause serious harm, or worse.

Like other prescription painkillers, one could say that Vicodin itself is innocent—it's only trying to help. The problem lies in the ways people use or misuse the

British actor Hugh Laurie portrays Dr. House on Fox's TV show *House*. As the brash doctor goes through each episode, he is seen popping little white pills and occasionally offers to share his medication with his patients.

trial, and a few near-losses of friends, the doctor was back to his usual game—and back on his usual drug.

drug. So don't let drug schedules, regulation, availability, and the "weakness" of prescription painkillers take
your focus off the facts. In the wrong hands, Vicodin has
the power to mess up lives—maybe for good.

4

OxyContin

"The sad part is, OxyContin really helps many people with serious pain. How the painkiller was hyped is inexcusable."

—Robert Trigaux (*St. Petersburg Times*, November 2003)

Not since the 1960s introduction of the tranquilizer Valium had so many Americans, young and old, known an addictive prescription drug by brand name. Then came OxyContin.

NEW RELIEF FROM PAIN

In 1996, a small Connecticut-based drug company called Purdue Pharma began marketing a new kind of pain reliever. Its only ingredient, the potent opioid

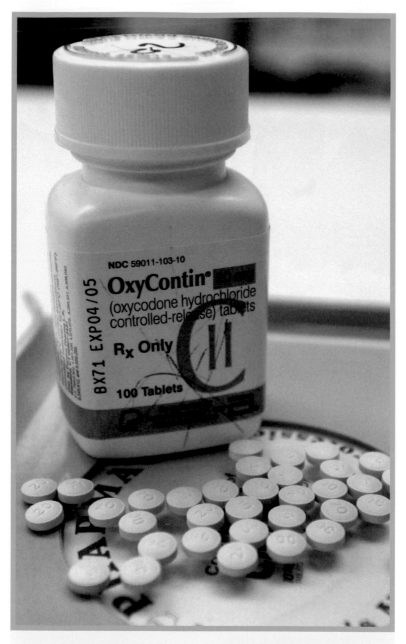

While OxyContin has proven to be an effective medication to help manage chronic pain, some people have discovered that crushing and sniffing or chewing the pills causes a euphoric high, similar to heroin.

oxycodone, had been used for years, but only in combination with other drugs. The new drug, called OxyContin, worked differently from other prescription painkillers. Once swallowed, the pill would release medication gradually over a course of 12 hours. This meant that pill users only had to take it twice a day to get effective, all-day pain relief. This made the risk of abuse and addiction, Purdue claimed, lower than with fast-acting painkillers.

Over the next few years, OxyContin's special design alone helped push sales of more than $1 billion a year. Like other strong opioids, OxyContin had been proposed at first as a treatment for the most severe types of pain, mainly that associated with cancer and surgery. It wasn't long, however, before Purdue's sales team was knocking on the doors of **general practitioners**, successfully peddling OxyContin as a remedy for other, more common types of pain. This may have been the first factor that led to the drug's troubles—and the reputation it may never shake.

WHAT HAPPENED?

How could a drug pitched as less addictive than others in its class become one of the most abused medications in history? For one thing, the very design that appealed to doctors and real patients turned out to be just as appealing to people looking for a high. They discovered that by chewing or crushing the pill (something the drug label strictly warns not to do), they could experience an instant, heroinlike high. They might snort it like cocaine, or mix it with water and inject it. This practice first became common in several communities in the Appalachian region of the United States, earning OxyContin the nickname "hillbilly heroin" in 2001. Although the abuse trend remained particularly popular in parts of Kentucky, West Virginia, and Tennessee, it soon seeped into other parts of the country as well.

Critics of Purdue Pharma argue that the company's broad advertising strategy for the drug—that is, selling it to general practitioners, rather than just cancer doctors, surgeons, and others specializing in pain—was the other part of the abuse equation. Although the Schedule II drug is technically more difficult to come by than

 ## YES, WE HAVE NO OXYCONTIN

Armored cars, steel vaults, and high-tech security systems are nothing new to bankers. And, thanks to a new kind of robbery in the early 2000s, these precautions have become pretty familiar to pharmacists, too.

In most cases, the thieves wouldn't demand a whole host of controlled substances, or even any cash. They just wanted one thing: OxyContin. "By having it, it's like having cash in your hand," said police Capt. Jim Thomas (of Weymouth, Massachusetts) to a *New York Times* reporter in 2001. "You can sell it easily on the street."

Some of these robberies were planned extremely well. Plagued by crimes, several pharmacies throughout New England, Appalachian states, and other areas scrambled to protect their people and their goods. Many pharmacists stopped keeping OxyContin in their stores. Instead, they would make it available by special order only. Window signs informing customers of this policy became common sights throughout high-risk regions. According to the online hydrocodone, some believe its frequency of prescription may have added to its availability within the general community. (A 2004 study by Congress, however, failed to prove this.) As millions continued to take the drug legally and as prescribed, mainly to treat moderate-to-severe chronic pain, others—addicts and dealers— were finding ways to beg, borrow, or steal it. At one time, OxyContin-related crimes and tragedies seemed to

journal *Pharmacy Times,* some pharmacies began storing OxyContin in vaults that only certain employees could enter. Other pharmacies installed safety glass through which the pharmacist could interact with customers. New alarm systems, surveillance cameras, and barred windows have also come into play.

For their part, medical drug companies have used strategies to help discourage theft. Some companies deliver OxyContin in armored trucks—sometimes accompanied by armed guards—and will monitor deliveries at every step.

The seriousness of the OxyContin abuse epidemic has come and gone. Still, the theft of prescription narcotics remains an ongoing problem. Even today, robberies seem to happen "all the time, but more in big cities and in 24-hour stores," says one Boston-area pharmacist. "I guess the only time you get scared is when you hear about it happening in a pharmacy near you—knowing that it could potentially *be* you."

Because of the high rates of OxyContin addiction in Kentucky, pharmacists like Carrie Cinnamond, seen here, have installed extra security measures in their stores. Cinnamond has cameras watching over her whole store.

make headlines on a regular basis. How bad did it get? Consider these actual reports:

> "Susanne Smith Bowers, age 44 of Asheville, NC, was arrested on March 8th and charged with one count of larceny by employee and two counts of possession of a Schedule II controlled substance. Bowers was employed as a pharmacist with K-Mart in Boone. An audit of the pharmacy led to Bowers being suspected of taking drugs from the pharmacy and further investigation led to Bowers being charged. She is alleged to have taken oxycodone and hydromorphone over a two-month period of time."
>
> —from the Web site for the town of Boone, North Carolina

"A New York man was arrested today on charges that he aided a May 24, 2001, armed robbery of the Veterans Affairs Medical Center pharmacy in Boston. . . . The complaint alleges that the robbers gained access to the pharmacy by posing as flower delivery men. Once inside, they brandished at least one shotgun and forced three employees into the pharmacy's narcotics vault, where the employees were tied up. The robbers then emptied OxyContin, morphine, dilaudid, methadone, Valium, and other drugs into duffle bags and fled. [Joshua E.] Friedman faces a thirty-two year prison sentence and a $250,000 fine if convicted of the crimes charged in the complaint."

—from a press release issued by U.S. Attorney's Office, Boston, July 24, 2001. Posted on state of Virginia's official Web site.

"An OxyContin dealer who sold what proved to be a fatal dose of the prescription painkiller was sentenced to 13 1/2 years in prison Tuesday. Robert Stallard was found guilty of felony murder in what is thought to be the country's first murder conviction involving the distribution of OxyContin, a potent narcotic that can be a blessing for people in pain and a curse for those who abuse it."

—from *The Roanoke Times*, August 29, 2001

"Attorney General J. Joseph Curran, Jr., announced today that Danielle Williams, 18, of the 1500 block of Ellamont Street, Baltimore, was charged in an 82-count indictment with possession with intent to distribute OxyContin and two other controlled dangerous substances. Williams was also charged with theft, fraud, and conspiracy. It is alleged that from June 2002 to December 2002, Williams uttered prescriptions using

Relatives and friends of the people who have died from OxyContin over-doses picket outside a courtroom in Abingdon, Virginia. In this small mountain town, the three executives of Purdue Pharma responsible for the deceptive promotion of OxyContin plead guilty to misleading the public about the drug.

the names and Medicaid numbers of actual Medicaid recipients, when in fact all of the prescriptions were fraudulent."

—from the office of the Attorney General of Maryland, February 13, 2003

Some doctors were also accused and even convicted of a variety of offenses related to giving out illegal prescriptions. This made the medical community nervous, leading many doctors to shy away from prescribing OxyContin at all. Not surprisingly, Purdue Pharma and its key players also found themselves in the hot seat,

BUSTED: THE DAY PURDUE PAID

On May 10, 2007, the company responsible for the manufacture and sales of OxyContin admitted something that
millions of patients, doctors, and people from government
drug agencies had long demanded to hear: The company
had misled people on purpose.

Purdue Frederick, the larger company that owns
OxyContin's maker Purdue Pharma, pleaded guilty to
charges of "misbranding" its product. Three of its executives pleaded guilty as well, and Purdue agreed to pay
$600 million in fines and payments for the crime.
Misbranding involves printing false or misleading information on labels and promoting a drug for unapproved use.
The executives, including the company's president, Michael
Friedman; its top lawyer, Howard R. Udell; and its former
medical director, Dr. Paul D. Goldenheim, agreed to pay
$34.5 million in fines all together. The company, however,
stated that the executives themselves did not know about
the misbranding, which Purdue admits occurred between
1995 and 2001. (This kind of misbranding charge can be
filed even when the accused people are unaware of the
activity.)

Part of the U.S. Food and Drug Administration's job
is to examine and approve the use of new medications.
When it approved the use of OxyContin, the FDA said that
the drug's design was "believed to reduce" its potential
to be abused. Yet, Purdue salesmen reportedly made
stronger statements to doctors who didn't quite believe
that. The prosecutors in the Purdue trial also said that the

(continues on page 58)

(continued from page 57)

company specifically trained its salespersons to help such doctors overcome concerns about addiction. In 2001, Purdue stopped these practices, but the company admits prior wrongdoing. "We accept responsibility for those past misstatements and regret they were made," stated a company spokesperson, according to an article in the *New York Times* on May 11, 2007.

More than three-quarters of the fines that Purdue must pay will be made to federal and state agencies, and the rest will settle lawsuits filed by patients. In another court decision a few days before its guilty plea, Purdue agreed to pay 26 states and the District of Columbia $19.5 million for lawsuits related to encouraging excessive prescription of OxyContin.

fighting off hundreds of lawsuits and submitting to a congressional investigation within a span of a few years. In a historic 2007 case, the company finally pled guilty to making false advertising claims.

A BITTER PILL

If there are two sides to every story, the story of Oxy-Contin is no exception. Despite the drug's bad reputation, there are plenty of people who see the drug as something far from criminal. These people include pain sufferers as well as professionals in the medical, criminology, and other fields. They see the drug for what it just may be: an important pain medication. And even with the drug's bad reputation, headlines such as "OxyContin Half-Truths Can Cause Suffering" and "Pain Patients Hurt by OxyContin Hype" are found on the Internet. These pro-OxyContin headlines show that the drug does have the power to do good.

According to the drug's supporters, the media frenzy surrounding the drug may be more harmful than the actual drug itself. "The constant stories in the media want to make OxyContin and Purdue Pharma the bad guys," wrote crime expert Susan R. Paisner in a 2002 opinion article in *The Pain Practitioner,* "all for a drug that has given hope and normalcy to countless chronic pain patients who had despaired of ever regaining either." Some people even largely blame the media for the epidemic of OxyContin abuse. Dr. B. Eliot Cole, former president of the American Academy of Pain Management, said in an interview, "Only a handful of really seasoned addicts knew about this medicine a year ago, but now, thanks to NBC, CBS, ABC, the *New York Times, Forbes, Time, U.S. News and World Report,* everyone knows. If this wasn't the manufacturing of madness, what is?"

Still, before accepting an OxyContin prescription, patients should discuss all risks, side effects, precautions, and other safety information with the doctor prescribing the drug. Vicodin or other fast-acting pain-killers may be prescribed for short- or long-term use, but OxyContin is not like that. OxyContin is usually reserved for severe, ongoing pain that lasts all day. Many patients with this kind of pain say OxyContin is what finally worked for them—and that's all that matters. In a 2007 article, the wife of a pain patient told *New York*

Times reporter Tina Rosenberg about the struggles that her husband, Ben, went through. "When Ben first went to [physician Ronald McIver, who is now in prison for illegal prescribing practices] and filled out the form on

 ## CLUB MED: OXYCONTIN

Like Vicodin, OxyContin has been named in connection with many celebrities' troubles, as these stories show.

Learning of a warrant for her arrest, singer/musician Courtney Love turned herself in for illegal possession of both OxyContin and Vicodin in February 2004. On October 3, 2003, she had called 911 to report that she may have overdosed on the drugs. She made the call just hours after smashing several windows of her ex-boyfriend's house. Love was arrested for being under the influence of a controlled substance. Since the incident, she has been in and out of court-ordered rehabilitation for crimes related to drugs and violence.

A week after Courtney Love's arrest, political commentator Rush Limbaugh publicly admitted on his radio show that he was addicted to prescription painkillers and was entering rehab. The admission came soon after police had received evidence that Limbaugh was illegally buying OxyContin, among other prescription narcotics.

In the spring of 2003, Jack Osbourne, singer Ozzie Osbourne's son and co-star of MTV's *The Osbournes*, entered two months of rehab for OxyContin addiction.

what he used to be able to do and what he could do now, he cried," Ben's wife said. "McIver said to him, 'I'm going to get you back to doing what you used to do.' And he did."

Jack Osbourne, son of rocker Ozzy Osbourne and former co-star of MTV's reality TV show *The Osbournes*, went to a rehabilitation treatment center for an addiction to prescription painkillers. In an interview with MTV News, he described his experiences with OxyContin and said that he was addicted instantly to the drug.

Describing the moment he surrendered to his problem, Osbourne told MTV News: "I was really loaded, and I just sat on my mom's bed, and I just said, 'I am going to go pack my bags, I'm, I'm ready to go. I want to go, I need to go.'"

5

Other Prescription Opioids

Today, pain sufferers wishing to try a medication have no shortage of options. In the shadows of the two most well-known painkillers are dozens more prescription narcotics—not as famous, maybe, but no less powerful. Here's an overview of a few of them.

MORPHINE: A TRUE ORIGINAL

Young people tend to be curious. Combine this trait with natural intelligence and drive, and your name might just make it into medical textbooks. Take the case of Friedrich Wilhelm Serturner (1783–1841), a German pharmacist's assistant. Serturner was fascinated by opium, which doctors had long been using to treat pain and other symptoms. To fulfill his curiosity about the drug, the uneducated 21-year-old began a series of scientific experiments. The result? The discovery of the "heart" of opium, which Serturner found had 10 times the effect of the pure processed plant. Serturner was able to separate the heart of this drug from all the other substances in opium. He named the new drug *morphine*, after Morpheus, the Greek god of dreams.

Since Serturner's discovery in 1805, morphine has been around for many important historical events, and many more everyday events. It has both eased the agony of battle wounds, and helped teething babies sleep better (a morphine-containing "soothing syrup" was once available for this). Morphine is so effective that it has remained something of a model drug. The effects and strength of new painkillers are still measured against this original opiate.

Morphine, one of the "strong" opioids, is one of the most common opioids used in hospitals. In fact, despite the development and sale of so many new painkillers, the medical use of morphine has doubled since 1998. Morphine has long been a preferred remedy for chest pain in patients in the hospital for a heart attack. This, however, is a use that has recently caused some concern. A 2005 Duke University study found that heart attack patients treated with morphine may have a nearly 50% higher risk of dying. Researchers plan to confirm their findings through a scientific study. In the meantime, they have advised doctors to use morphine in heart attack patients only as a last resort.

Another area of medicine that uses morphine is *palliative* care, or end-of-life care. This involves helping patients with **terminal** illnesses live as comfortably as possible, usually in their own homes. Many cancers can cause chronic and sometimes unbearable pain that is relieved only by the strongest medications. Although several types of opioids may work, doctors usually

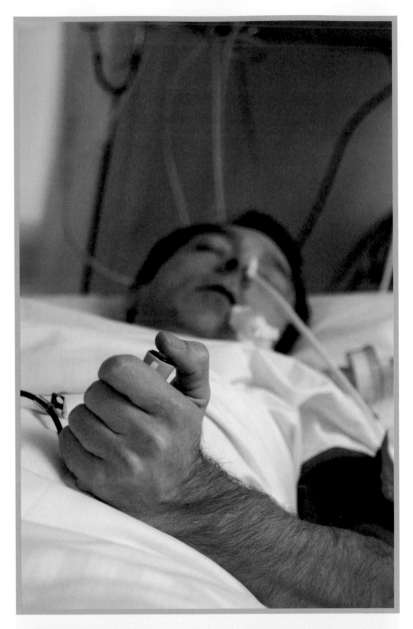

After surgery, doctors sometimes prescribe morphine to ease a patient's discomfort. In this photo, a patient holds a button that, when pushed, administers limited doses of morphine to be released into his IV. This allows the patient to use the drug only as needed.

prescribe morphine. In addition to providing pain relief, morphine can help these patients feel relaxed and breathe more easily.

In the past, morphine was almost always delivered through an injection. In fact, the invention of the hypodermic syringe in the mid-1800s became a major piece of the drug's history. Today, morphine also exists as a fluid to swallow, as time-released capsules and tablets,

 # CIVIL WAR . . . ON DRUGS?

When war broke out between the North and South of the United States in 1861, soldiers had at least one advantage over those who had fought in past battles. Civil War soldiers had a means of instant pain relief. Scottish doctor Alexander Wood had invented the hypodermic syringe only eight years before the war began. A hypodermic syringe is a needle that can be used to inject medicine into a person's bloodstream. Its invention was just in time for the fast delivery of morphine to the tens of thousands of soldiers who crowded army hospital tents, or who lay dying in battlefields.

Still, there was a serious downside. So many soldiers became addicted to the drug that morphine addiction earned the names "army disease" and "soldiers' disease." It's not certain which is most to blame: the invention, the war, the widespread availability of opiates, or a combination of those causes. But one thing is certain: The problem of morphine addiction among the general population skyrocketed throughout the rest of the 1800s.

and as suppositories (tablets inserted into the rectum). It is sold under brand names such as MS Contin and Oramorph. Like OxyContin, morphine pills should never be crushed or chewed. Doing so could instantly release poisonous amounts of the drug into a person's body. As with any opioid drug, anyone taking morphine or prescribing it to someone else should be aware of possible serious side effects and signs of overdose.

CODEINE: THE OTHER OPIATE

Friedrich Wilhelm Serturner's work was not appreciated overnight. In fact, it took years for the medical community to pay real attention to what this young man, whom nobody knew, had done. Once they did, however, it wasn't long before scientists throughout Europe started taking apart the poppy plant to see what other promising treasures it held. In 1832, French chemist Pierre-Jean Robiquet extracted a second substance from the opium poppy. This new substance had traits similar to those of morphine. It was codeine, and Robiquet's discovery marked the birth of a new painkiller.

Today, codeine is the most widely used true opiate in the world. But codeine is found only in small amounts in the poppy plant. Because of this, most codeine used in the United States is actually **synthetic**—it is synthesized from morphine. Although medications containing mainly or only codeine do exist, the ingredient is used much more often in combination with other drugs, such as acetaminophen. Depending on a few things— including the amount of codeine a drug contains— medications containing codeine fall anywhere between Schedule II and Schedule V.

Codeine is similar to hydrocodone (brand name Vicodin). Think of codeine as the "natural" Vicodin. In fact, codeine is the substance used as the base for making hydrocodone. This makes hydrocodone an opioid that is partly synthetic. (Oxycodone, made from a third natural opiate called thebaine, is also partly synthetic.) Codeine combinations are weak opioids, compared to some other drugs. Because of this, drugs made from codeine are usually prescribed for mild to moderately severe pain that is not expected to last very long. When acetaminophen or an NSAID is not enough for a patient's pain, acetaminophen with codeine is often the next drug tried. Codeine-based medications are available as liquids to swallow, as tablets, or as capsules.

Like its synthetic cousin hydrocodone, codeine is also prescribed for the treatment of coughs. There are dozens of prescription cough medications today containing codeine. In general, these drugs are saved for the treatment of chronic, dry coughs that aren't caused by a serious respiratory illness.

Unfortunately, the catch that's true for Vicodin is also true for codeine—and has been for decades. Since codeine is weak compared to other drugs, and because it has many medical uses, it is often widely available. And that means it's easy to abuse. For as long as people have been taking codeine legally, others have been abusing it.

Doctors and pharmacists are trained to use caution when prescribing and distributing medicines that contain codeine—particularly cough syrups. "Sometimes they won't give me the codeine syrup," said a "patient" interviewed for a 1999 study by the Texas Commission on Alcohol and Drug Abuse. "When that happens, I'll go back to the doctor and say it hasn't worked and I need something stronger."

ENTER OPIOIDS: SYNTHETIC RELIEF FOR REAL PAIN

The isolation of morphine, codeine, and thebaine opened the doors to a whole new field—and new hope.

Scientists could now study the traits of the opiates and therefore synthesize them. This created a whole new group of pain-relieving drugs. In addition to Vicodin and OxyContin, pain patients regularly find names such as Percocet (acetaminophen and oxycodone), Percodan (aspirin and oxycodone), Demerol (meperidine), Darvon (propoxyphene), and Dilaudid (hydromorphone) on their prescription bottles, or on packets they take home when released from the hospital.

Are all opioids the same? Yes and no. All opioids block pain signals being sent to the brain. All opioids cause sleepiness, and all of them have the same general side effects, as well as the potential for addiction. Beyond that, some are stronger than others, and each may have traits that make it preferred—or off-limits—for certain people or circumstances. For example:

The use of Demerol, one of the oldest synthetic opioids, has declined since the introduction of other and possibly safer painkillers. Demerol was once among the most common narcotics used in IVs after surgery. It acts on pain for only a short time and can be dangerous if continued for more than a few days, because processes in the body can produce a toxin from it. Although its pill form is still sometimes prescribed for moderate pain, Demerol is mainly used in health-care facilities for pain associated with medical procedures.

Percocet is an extremely common opioid. It is used as an alternative to medicines containing codeine and is available in several different strengths. But doctors might avoid prescribing Percocet (or any drug containing acetaminophen) to patients with liver problems or a history of alcoholism. This is because of acetaminophen's possibly toxic effects on the liver. Any patient taking Percocet must carefully monitor dosages, keeping in mind the risks of acetaminophen and of narcotics.

Thanks in part to concerns over OxyContin, doctors have been prescribing hydromorphone (brand name Dilaudid) more than four times as often since the beginning of the 2000s. Dilaudid is used most often for moderate to severe pain. Scientific evidence suggests that it is six to seven times more potent than morphine, and has a higher potential to be abused than other Schedule II narcotics. Because of this, other treatments should be

 EMERGENCY: SIGNS OF TOO MUCH

An overdose of any substance can be dangerous, but it's a sure thing with narcotics. Too much of an opioid can stop a person's breathing or heart, potentially killing him or her. Key signs of opioid overdose include:

- Extreme drowsiness or seeming "out of it"
- Deep sleep
- Pauses in breathing during sleep (called sleep apnea)
- Slowed breathing or heart rate
- Muscle weakness ("spaghetti arms")
- Cold, wet skin
- Tiny pupils

If you suspect that you or a friend has overdosed on an opioid, call 911 or get to a hospital emergency room immediately. Suspected opioid overdoses are usually treated with a drug called naloxone, given through an IV. Naloxone works quickly to reverse the effects of opioids.

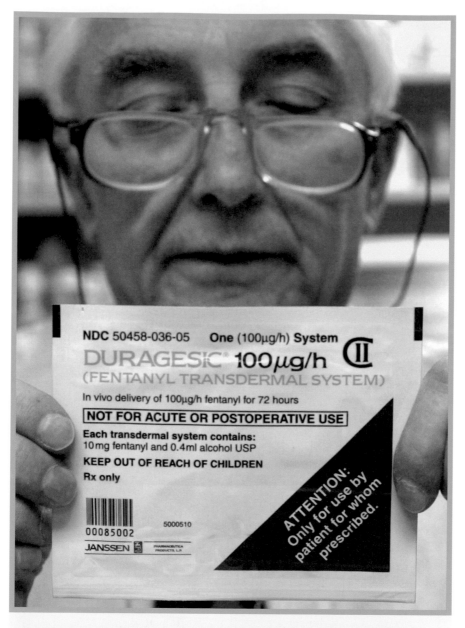

Temple University Hospital pharmacist Norman Folkman holds Dura-gesic, a skin patch that releases the painkiller fetanyl into the bloodstream. Some federal officials believe the abuse of Duragesic is on the rise due to the crackdown of OxyContin abuse. A rising number of deaths have been attributed to the drug.

considered for anyone who has never taken an opioid or who has a history of drug abuse. The officials who keep watch over drugs have already taken careful actions with hydromorphone. In September 2004, the FDA approved a medicine known as Palladone, which contained hydromorphone. In 2005, Palladone was taken out of stores when it was discovered that drinking alcohol could cause dangerously rapid release of the drug in the body.

In 1990, the FDA approved a drug featuring a clever way to deliver pain-relief medicine: through the skin. Duragesic is a skin patch that releases a dose of fentanyl slowly and steadily. Fentanyl is an opioid that has been used since the 1960s as a pain reliever and as a drug to numb patients before surgery. Like other strong opioids, Duragesic (and its generic version) is meant for long-term use by people who have chronic, constant, and severe pain. Patients who are thinking about using a fentanyl patch should be *opioid-tolerant.* This means that they have used other, weaker opioids with no serious problems. Cancer patients and others have found much-needed relief with skin patches. The patches are often prescribed in addition to opioid pills or liquids that are used for sudden outbursts of pain.

In developing new opioids, a goal has been to keep side effects and possibilities for addiction to a minimum. But although a patient might respond better to one opioid than another, chemists have not yet created a narcotic that has no risk. That's where medical science leaves off, and personal responsibility begins.

6

Misuse
and Addiction

"Four out of 10 teens agree that prescription medicines are much safer to use than illegal drugs, even if
they are not prescribed by a doctor."

—from *Teens and Prescription Drugs*, an analysis
by the Office of National Drug Control Policy

With beliefs like this so common, it shouldn't be
any wonder that prescription drug abuse and
related medical emergencies are on the rise. As previ-
ous chapters have made clear, the same medications
that have been called miraculous for their painkilling
powers have been criticized for their powers of destruc-
tion. The difference is in how—and by whom—they
are used.

DRUGS OF THE DAY

"'Please,' I said to the harried waitress, 'I only want a glass of water.' I fumbled for the pills in my purse . . . I closed my eyes and tried to catch my breath. How long have I been living like this?"

The above text is an excerpt from Barbara Gordon's bestselling memoir *I'm Dancing as Fast as I Can* (1979). The pills to which she refers are the tranquilizer Valium (generic name diazepam), a kind of drug known as a benzodiazepine. And "living like this" means popping some Valium just to get through a day. In courageously publicizing her personal journey, Gordon, at that time a successful television writer and producer, helped bring about awareness of the problem of prescription drug addiction.

As Gordon's story demonstrates, the epidemic is nothing new. All that changes through time are the specific drugs of choice. Even well before the introduction of Valium and other benzodiazepines, doctors often treated anxiety and insomnia (the inability to fall asleep) with drugs from another class of sedatives. These sedatives, known as barbiturates, are strong, highly addictive, and possibly deadly if mixed with alcohol. Barbiturates all but slipped out of medical use once Valium came on the scene in 1963. By the 1970s, Valium was among the most widely prescribed drugs in America. By the time people realized its potential for addiction, many users—mostly women—had become hooked.

Doctors still prescribe benzodiazepines and these drugs are still widely abused. But the class of prescription drugs most often associated with addiction, crime, hospitalizations, and death are the opioids. According to the National Institute on Drug Abuse, benzodiazepines accounted for 100,784 emergency room visits in

2002. That same year, opioids were the reason for about 119,000 visits.

The answer to why this happens may partly lie in the fast growth of the pain medication business. The medical community has recognized pain as a serious, life-changing condition in its own right, and not just a symptom of another disease. As a result, the pharmaceutical companies that make drugs have placed painkillers among their top priorities for development and sales. A real need for medicine led to a business worth billions of dollars. It also made it easier for people to obtain painkillers. These conditions, unfortunately, can help set the stage for misuse and addiction.

Peoples' false beliefs also likely play a part in the abuse of prescription drugs. Young people in particular don't seem to see much of a problem with abusing painkilling drugs. According to *Teens and Prescription Drugs*, nearly one third of teens believe that prescription pain relievers are not addictive. After all, marijuana, cocaine, and Ecstasy are not stored in a family's medicine cabinet, much less in a bottle from a pharmacy. But that's where prescription drugs are found. "Rich kids with good reputations who wouldn't smoke pot, take Vicodin because they think it doesn't make them druggies," says teen Meena Hartenstein in her commentary on NPR's *Youth Radio*. Many times, narcotics might even be legally given to a teen, since doctors routinely prescribe these drugs after wisdom teeth surgery.

In short, teens may wonder how something legal, common, and helpful could possibly be so bad. But if you think about it, cars fit that description, too. Yet, cars kill more than 35,000 people in the United States every year—with the help of their drivers, of course. The same can be said for painkillers: they are helpful tools, but when not used safely, they can kill.

DANGER IN DOSAGES

Think of a medicine prescription as a sort of driver's license. Although neither a driver's license, nor a drug prescription, guarantees safety, that piece of paper is necessary—and for good reason.

Both the doctor and the patient have responsibilities when deciding to start treatment with an opioid: A health-care provider issuing a prescription must examine the patient. He or she must have extensive information about the patient, including current condition(s), health history, medications, allergies, and more. A patient with a prescription for a particular narcotic must be found to have significant pain, but also to have no health or personal factors that might make the drug a risky choice for him or her. In other words, what's safe for one person may well be dangerous—or deadly—for another. Michigan State University professor John Thornburg warned about the dangers of this when he spoke to a reporter from the university's student newspaper, *The State News*. "You may not have an accurate diagnosis and may not know what the drug will do," said Thornburg, who teaches pharmacology and toxicology, and is a doctor at the school's health clinic. "You may get more than you bargained for." The fact is, unless a doctor has given you a prescription, you just don't know.

Addiction is, for sure, a risk with any opioid. But it certainly isn't the only one. When you don't know how a drug will affect you, even one use of the drug can have tragic consequences. Depending on your age, weight, health conditions, and other factors, one or two pills can slow your breathing to a lethal point. This risk increases tremendously if you have alcohol or certain other drugs in your system at the same time. *The State News* gives an example of an MSU student found dead in his home in February 2005. Medical reports showed

R&B singer Gerald Levert died in 2006 from an accidental overdose of prescription painkillers. Levert suffered from chronic pain, and he had combined over-the-counter medications with prescribed painkillers, including Percocet and Vicodin. In recent years, misuse of prescription medications has led to a sharp increase in the number of overdose deaths in the United States.

he had died accidentally from a combination of hydrocodone and methadone, another opioid.

Other stories illustrate that the dangers aren't limited to recreational use or even just to prescription drug combinations. R&B singer Gerald Levert suffered from a painful shoulder problem and respiratory illness. Levert died in 2006 from a combination of prescription painkillers, the anxiety medication Xanax, and two nonprescription allergy medications. The drugs triggered a heart attack as Levert slept. According to a report from the U.S. Centers for Disease Control and Prevention (CDC), deaths from accidental drug interactions rose 68% between 1999 and 2004, and "prescription drugs, especially prescription painkillers, are driving the prolonged increase."

Even if a prescription drug user's physical health is not damaged, there are other problems to consider. Under the influence of drugs, a person is more likely to take risks, be violent or commit other crimes, or be in an accident. And since using or possessing prescription drugs without a prescription is a crime, a person who is doing so can also face legal trouble. If recreational use turns into addiction, a person's friendships, family life, school achievement, and entire future are at stake. Keep in mind: You can't become addicted to something you choose to never try.

LIES OPIOIDS TELL: "I WAS SUPERWOMAN"

As a college student in the 1960s, Mary P. (not her real name), now a grandmother living in Massachusetts, was "totally pure" in terms of substance use. She had never had a cup of coffee, let alone alcohol or drugs. This might be, in part, why an over-the-counter pain reliever containing caffeine affected her like it did. She began taking the pain reliever for migraine headaches, but it wasn't quite enough. "If it was a true migraine, the medicine wouldn't touch it," she recalled. "But I noticed that for minor headaches, it would not only relieve the headache, but it gave me a tremendous caffeine rush." Since the drug was not helping her more severe headaches, Mary visited her campus health center, where she was quickly prescribed the painkiller Fiorinal with codeine. It was a day Mary will never forget. It marked, after all, the beginning of a slow but sure descent into the world of opioid addiction.

A story like Mary's could have happened yesterday. According to the National Institute on Drug Abuse, millions of people each year use prescription medications, especially painkillers, for reasons other than medical ones. Although some of these people may be using the drugs recreationally and without a prescription, others begin abusing drugs they have been honestly prescribed. This is often the first sign of addiction. Some people report that in the early stages, the drug seemed to give them a lift they'd never experienced before. "It was a great feeling," a recovering Vicodin addict named Dave (not his real name) told the *Detroit Metro Times* in a 2001 article. "I went home and started vacuuming the house, which is something I never did." Mary's early experience was similar. "When I took the codeine, I was Superwoman," she said. "I loved everybody. I loved doing every chore. I was more of a joy to be around." She was also in denial, she later admitted. "I didn't dream of how far gone I was," she said. Dave's addiction drove him to seek Vicodin on the streets—sometimes spending thousands of dollars at a time—while nearly destroying his marriage and his once-profitable business.

Medical research and experience show that addiction is unlikely for people who take pain relievers exactly as prescribed. "Studies show that 10% of men and 5% of women are born with a genetic predisposition [meaning they inherit the trait from their parents and

NOT ADDICTED, JUST DEPENDENT

A woman has had lingering pain since being in a car accident last year. Ibuprofen hasn't cut it, even with the addition of hypnosis and massage. When her doctor recommends an opioid, a look of concern comes over the woman's face. If she starts a narcotic, she asks, won't she get used the drug and need more and more to dull the pain? The doctor responds in a casual way that, yes, that's probably exactly what will happen. Then he takes out his prescription pad.

This doctor is not sending his patient off to become a drug addict. As he goes on to explain to the patient, there are major differences among addiction, tolerance, and physical dependence. The fact is, many people who begin taking a prescription narcotic may eventually become tolerant to the drug's effects. This means that, as the patient above described, their bodies may stop responding to a given amount of the drug, and therefore they will require more. Some people also may become physically dependent on the drug. If they suddenly stop taking it, they might experience uncomfortable symptoms called withdrawal. These symptoms can include sweating, muscle twitching, nausea and vomiting, and more. Tolerance, physical dependence, and withdrawal are purely physical and go along with the ingredients of certain drugs. This is not just limited to opioids: Even some blood pressure medications can cause physical dependence, and they have possible withdrawal symptoms that can actually be dangerous. Patients who develop tolerance or physical dependence can work with their doctors on making simple changes to their treatment plan.

(continues on page 80)

(continued from page 79)

Addiction, on the other hand, is a problem with the mind and with behavior. In general, a person who is addicted to a substance will do whatever it takes to get it, and will feel as though he can't go through life without it. He will see the drug as more important than other things in his life. In this way, the addicted person often risking losing or destroying the things in his life that are truly important, such as friendships, family relationships, and career.

It is important to note, however, that the fear of becoming an addict should not stop someone from seeking out the best pain relief possible. Tolerance and physical dependence do not make a person an addict. A pain patient can avoid the dangers of addiction by proper communicating with a doctor, in addition to taking personal responsibility.

grandparents] to become addicted to substances, be it alcohol or drugs," explained addiction specialist Dr. Brian McCarroll in the *Metro Times* article. "There's something wrong with the pleasure centers of their brains compared to other people's." It's true that most people who use prescription painkillers over an extended period of time will come to depend on the drug, but this is not the same as being addicted. In fact, so many peoples' fear of addiction has some experts concerned that opioids are not prescribed often enough for patients who need them. The key, experts say, is effective communication between the doctor and patient. As Dr. Richard Brown of the University of Wisconsin Medical School told *FDA*

Consumer magazine: "Patients should be honest about their substance abuse history because then it tells me to watch them even more closely."

For Mary, now drug-free for nearly 20 years, those Superwoman days were far outnumbered by the miserable ones that followed. After a failed attempt at rehab and seven more years of using, "my addiction had progressed to the point where . . . nothing worked for me anymore," she said. "I hated myself, and I lost all my self-respect. Finally, I surrendered—and was totally willing to change."

PRESCRIPTION MONITORING PROGRAMS: NO OPIOID GOES UNCHECKED

In at least two-thirds of the country, a lot is being done about the problem of prescription drug addiction and misuse. As of November 2006, 33 states were set to establish Prescription Monitoring Programs (PMPs). These are statewide systems that track the prescription of controlled substances and how they are given to patients. Every time pharmacies in these states fill a prescription for a Schedule II drug (and/or lesser-controlled substances in some states), information is entered into an electronic database, which can be accessed by a certain state agency. When the agency spots possible "red flags"—signs that a patient is taking advantage of doctors or pharmacies to get more drugs—the agency can contact the appropriate sources of help, such as a patient's doctor(s) or pharmacist(s), or law enforcement.

The program is also a resource for doctors. If they have any concerns about a particular patient, they may request a patient history report before prescribing an opioid. "Forged and fraudulent prescriptions can remain unreported or undetected unless states have a program or agency committed to addressing the issue," said

(continues on page 84)

"MY MEDICINE FELL DOWN THE SINK" . . . AND OTHER NICE TRIES

A drug addict may stop at nothing to get his or her hands on more drugs. In the case of prescription drugs, the tricks people try often happen at the pharmacy counter. Melissa Ryan (not her real name) is a Boston-area pharmacist employed by a national drugstore company. Below are her descriptions of the fraud attempts that she most often sees on the job—and why they usually don't work.

1. Fake prescriptions. Stealing the special pads of paper that doctors use to write prescriptions is a relatively common crime. If a criminal actually manages to get drugs this way, Ryan said, the success usually doesn't last. "Sometimes we get e-mails from different pharmacies saying, 'if you get a script [prescription] from this particular M.D. [doctor], double-check it, because somebody is writing prescriptions under his name."

2. Photocopied prescriptions. Go the copy route; end up with zero—drugs, that is. "This woman had a script for some form of oxycodone," Ryan recalled. "She dropped it off, and then I saw [a note] in her profile. [Pharmacies keep information on current and former customers.] I think what happened is she had pulled it off before and gotten away with it, and they didn't realize it until after she left. I was fortunate enough to have that note, and right when I looked at the prescription, I could see it was clearly a photocopied signature."

3. Altered prescriptions. As Ryan has learned, one phone call can defeat this technique. "I had one lady who changed the quantity on a script for Vicodin," she said. "I called the doctor on an unrelated note [about the prescription], but then also wanted to verify. I said, 'I have this script here for 15,' and the office said, 'yeah, you can rip that up, because he wrote it for 5.'"

4. Doctor shopping. Some people manage to get multiple prescriptions for a drug by appealing to a number of health-care providers. Then they'll shop various pharmacies to get these prescriptions filled. "What they'll do is only use their insurance card at one of the pharmacies, and at the rest of the pharmacies, they'll pretend they don't have insurance," Ryan said. In doing this, the person will think he is avoiding a paper trail of evidence. "The frustrating part is a lot of these people are Medicaid patients, so we are paying for their insurance, and yet they are going and paying out of pocket for drugs."

5. Laughable lines. "[The drug] either fell down the sink, or it was stolen—that one's sometimes accompanied by a [fake] police report," Ryan shares. "Or, a lot of times, they are 'leaving for vacation on a plane in one hour and need their medication right now.' Yeah, stolen, vacation, and sink—those are the biggest ones."

(continued from page 81)
Regina B. Schofield, assistant attorney general for the Office of Justice Programs.

The purpose of PMPs isn't necessarily to "bust" patients or doctors. In fact, the data collected can help possible drug abusers to get treatment. For example, when a patient is shown to be "doctor shopping"—obtaining prescriptions for the same drug from multiple doctors—officials may contact the doctors directly. Doctors can then help patients get help, whether it be a drug treatment program or just better management for their pain. Some experts believe that if PMPs operate as they are supposed to, there will be fewer drug arrests because patients will get help before they get into real trouble.

The proven power of PMPs in stopping prescription drug abuse is somewhat debated. There does seem to be evidence of positive effects. For example, the Office of Justice Programs reported that the five states with the lowest rate of OxyContin prescriptions are states that have PMPs. On the other hand, the five states with the highest rates of OxyContin prescriptions do not have PMPs. A 2006 study conducted by Robert Twillman, head of the Kansas Pain Initiative, agreed with this finding. But Twillman had an additional note: In states where there are fewer prescriptions for OxyContin (a Schedule II drug), there are more prescriptions for Vicodin (a Schedule III drug). Twillman makes the point that the states where OxyContin and other Schedule II opioids have become scarcer are states that keep watch only Schedule II drugs. A study published in 2005 found no significant difference at all in the number of prescriptions in PMP and non-PMP states. Still, doctors have generally reported that PMPs are helpful, and some states have done studies that determined that the programs work as they should.

7

Getting Help

One person's addiction may have started when taking an opioid after her surgery. For someone else, a bottle with leftover pills might have sparked a curiosity. Yet another person may recall taking the drugs for fun, just wanting to fit in with "friends." The stories of people addicted to prescription drugs may be more varied than those of other substance abusers. In the end, however, addiction is addiction. But there is a way out.

"I WAS SO NUMB TO EVERYTHING . . . AND DIDN'T CARE"

It's hard to face the truth in the face of constant lies. It's even harder when the lies are coming from within yourself—or, more accurately, from an addiction that has overtaken you. It's no wonder people sometimes

85

refer to addiction as a "demon." That's what it is like. Most experts, including those from the U.S. National Institute on Drug Abuse, agree that addiction is a disease, and not a personal flaw or weakness.

Because addiction messes so much with a person's mind, recognizing when to get help can be a major challenge. That's why friends and family are often the first to see the problem. Unfortunately, no one can force an addict to get help. He or she must recognize the need and have the desire to do something about it.

Many people who have successfully stopped abusing prescription drugs remember exactly when—and why— they admitted to themselves that they needed help. It may have been a particular moment, or just the general state of their lives finally sinking in. "I was so numb to everything in life and didn't care," writes a poster to an online addiction support forum. "I became so depressed about all of the lying, forgery and everything that I wanted to die." In some cases, nearly dying is the very event that does it. "The fact that I had a problem came to a head when I took an overdose of about 40 tablets and found myself in the hospital," reads a quote on the Web site of the Foundation for a Drug-Free World, a drug treatment and education program.

Addiction remains a somewhat mysterious disease. Medical experts continue to explore the workings of addiction, with the goals of better identification, treatment, and possible prevention. The gray areas are even grayer with prescription drugs, since the line between legal use and recreational use can be hard to see—and even harder to prove. Despite this, there is guidance that can help people recognize prescription drug addiction in themselves or someone they love. General signs include:

- being preoccupied with prescriptions (obtaining and filling them)

- appearing to take pills frequently (as witnessed by friends or family)
- going through a lot of pills in a short period of time (determining this might require daily counting of missing pills)
- having several bottles of pills around at once
- taking pills when there is little or no pain to treat
- taking someone else's prescribed pills
- showing or experiencing mood swings or unusual irritability
- stealing, borrowing money, or having unexplained financial troubles
- showing a decline in school or work performance
- friends or family expressing anger or hurt because of drug-related behavior
- feeling a loss of control because of drug use

None of these signs, especially alone, automatically means someone has a drug problem. But if you notice any of them in yourself or someone else, consider the possibility that addiction may be the problem.

"I DIDN'T KNOW WHERE TO TURN"

Deciding that you want to stop using drugs—and recognizing that you can't do it on your own—is a major step and a strong beginning. In fact, the addiction support group Alcoholics Anonymous awards a medallion called a "desire chip" to new members who simply express the desire to stop drinking for the next 24 hours.

The next step is to reach out to one of the many resources, from major organizations to caring friends, who are there to help you. Some people might feel overwhelmed by the broad concept of "getting help." If you have a trusted friend or relative with whom you feel comfortable talking about your problem, this can be a good place to start. Tell the person you want to stop, and ask him or her to support your decision and help you take action. You can also turn to another trusted adult in your life, such as a teacher, coach, school counselor, or religious leader. He or she can help point you in right direction.

Most people need professional help to overcome addiction. Seeking this kind of help is *not* a sign of weakness. On the contrary, it's the best thing a person can do if he or she has a drug problem. There are countless organizations and programs that exist for the purpose of helping people with drug addiction. Locate one that is right for you in one of these ways:

- Ask your regular doctor or a local hospital for information on resources in your area.
- Check the yellow pages of your phone book under "Drug Abuse Treatment" or "Mental Health Services."
- Contact the Substance Abuse Treatment Facility Locator (a service of the Substance Abuse and Mental Health Services Administration) at 1–800–662-HELP or http://findtreatment.samhsa.gov.
- Visit the Web site of Narcotics Anonymous at www.na.org. This can assist you in finding a local group and offer helpful information.
- Try a general Internet search on prescription drug addiction. This can open up a world of treatment options—and provide reassurance that you are far from alone. As a woman who posted on an addiction support site shared: "I knew I needed help but didn't know where to turn. I looked online and found this website,

posted a cry for help and got a reply saying what I needed to do."

If you think a family member or friend might be addicted, let him or her know you are concerned. If you are unsure how to go about this or worried about how the person might react, get advice from a mental-health professional with experience in addiction. (You can start looking for one using the same resources described above.)

WHAT WILL HAPPEN NEXT?

You want help, and you've found it. But what does it take to stop using drugs? For most opioid addicts, the first part of a treatment program is **detoxification**, sometimes simply called detox. This generally takes place in a treatment center, which, depending on location, cost, and other factors, may be something like a hospital (or actually be part of a hospital), a large home, or even a nice hotel.

The main reason it is necessary to go through detox in a supervised medical setting is withdrawal. If a person who is physically dependent on a narcotic just stops taking the drug all at once, he or she will likely get very sick and experience a lot of unpleasant effects. Health-care providers at treatment centers are trained to help patients stop taking drugs very slowly, to lessen withdrawal symptoms as much as possible. Mental health professionals are also very much involved, to help people cope with the process of stopping drug use. The usual length of the detox period for opioid users is about a week, although through a newer method known as "rapid detox," it's possible for doctors to detoxify an addict in a matter of hours.

(continues on page 92)

DETOXIFIED, IN SIX HOURS OR LESS?

It's well established that using medications, including certain narcotics, can improve the chances of success for people trying to overcome an opioid addiction. Another technique, known as "rapid detox" or "ultra-rapid detox," takes the medication intervention a step further. With rapid detox, the patient is placed under general anesthesia (the kind that makes him fall asleep), as if he were undergoing surgery. While asleep, the patient is given a drug called naltrexone, which, like the opioid treatments, helps block the part of the brain responsible for drug cravings. The patient awakes after four to six hours.

Rapid detox was developed in the early 1990s as a way to help people detox faster and with less discomfort. Many treatment programs now offer the method. Since its introduction, however, rapid detox has been closely examined by medical organizations. In a 2005 study published in the *Journal of the American Medical Association* (JAMA), it was found that there was "no advantage" of detox using anesthesia when compared to other methods that used medications. "Although providers advertise anesthesia-assisted detox as a fast and painless method to kick opiate addiction, the evidence does not support those statements," said lead researcher Dr. Eric Collins, from the College of Physicians and Surgeons of Columbia University. "Patients should consider the many risks associated with this approach, including fluid accumulation in the lungs, metabolic complications of diabetes, and a worsening of underlying bipolar illness, as well as other potentially serious adverse events."

Dr. Lance Gooberman, seen here, invented naltrexone, an implant medication designed to decrease the cravings for narcotics and alcohol. While it may reduce the physical effects of withdrawal, it does not treat the mental or emotional aspects of addiction.

Countless Web sites for detox programs tell it differently. "Rapid detox at Florida Detox has proven to be safe, compassionate, and more scientific than traditional drug detox," reads one home page, which also boasts support for its program by celebrity psychologist Dr. Phil. "We have successfully treated over 4,000 patients from Europe and throughout the United States."

So for someone desperate for help with addiction, could rapid detox be the way to go? It depends on a number of factors, from medical conditions to cost (the procedure isn't cheap). The bottom line: Patients should work closely with their doctors—and their families—to determine which treatment strategy is best for them.

(continued from page 89)

After detox, the patient moves on to the rehabilitation phase of treatment, or "rehab." This usually takes place at the same facility, but it can sometimes be a day program that does not require the patient to stay at the center overnight. Rehab is when the detoxified addict begins to reclaim his or her life. Addiction often leaves a person feeling afraid, ashamed, confused, and unsure of where to go from that point. His or her job, relationships, and other areas of importance might have been seriously affected by the drug use. Rehab programs help people cope with difficult emotions, get back on track, and essentially discover a new way of living.

RECOVERY ROAD

The phrase "road to recovery" really doesn't apply to drug addiction. Many people believe that, in the case of addiction, recovery *is* the road. In other words, recovery is an active, ongoing journey that continues for life. After leaving rehab, many people continue to attend local meetings sponsored by Narcotics Anonymous (NA). They can find support and encouragement from other people there who are also recovering from narcotic addiction.

Like the well-known support program Alcoholics Anonymous (AA), NA follows a 12-step program that focuses on spirituality and assessment of one's own actions and behaviors. To succeed in the program, a person must first admit he or she has a problem that is beyond his or her control. What the person *can* control is getting better. "Put it this way," said Mary P., the recovering codeine addict, "what a social worker told me was, 'you're not responsible for your addiction, but you are responsible for your recovery.' And I always remembered that."

OPIOIDS FOR TREATING ADDICTION

Drug detoxification can be an unpleasant experience. The reason can be summarized in one word: withdrawal. Someone with a serious drug problem, particularly to the opiate heroin, may develop a range of symptoms when the drug is stopped. This can be anything from insomnia (the inability to sleep) and cold flashes to diarrhea, vomiting, and bone pain. There are ways medical professionals help reduce these symptoms, or at least make them easier to handle. For example, they carefully monitor the speed at which the patient stops using the drug. They also provide mental-health counseling, and, sometimes, give the patient more narcotics.

As surprising as it sounds, for decades, addiction specialists have been using the synthetic opioid methadone as a treatment for heroin addiction. Today, two other "treatment narcotics," levo alphacetylmethadol (LAAM) and buprenorphine, are also used. And they're not just used to combat heroin. These drugs may also be used to help patients come off of any number of opioids, including oxycodone, hydrocodone, and morphine. They work by satisfying the person's physical dependence on opioids, thus helping lessen withdrawal symptoms. At the same time, they block the high of the heroin (or other drug) still in the body. The use of methadone—itself addictive and potentially dangerous—for this purpose is sometimes a topic of debate. Still, these treatments are approved by the FDA and generally supported by the medical community in appropriate cases.

Betty Ford, seen here with her husband President Gerald Ford, spoke openly about her addiction to prescription painkillers and alcohol with the American public. She also helped establish one of the most famous rehabilitation centers in the United States: the Betty Ford Center in Rancho Mirage, California.

As any recovering addict would surely tell you, getting clean and staying clean is not easy. But as he or she also would also probably say that it is possible to achieve. TeensHealth.com, a Web site developed by the Nemours Foundation, offers these tips:

- Tell family members and friends that you have decided to stop using drugs. Tell them you would appreciate their sensitivity and support. You might ask a particular person (or more than one) if you may call him or her if you're having a tough time.

- Stop hanging around with people who use drugs. This may be hard, but fighting the urge to use with them around will be harder.
- Try to avoid places and events where you know there will be drugs.
- Have a plan in case you find yourself in a situation involving drugs. For example, you might call a parent or other trusted adult and use an established code phrase. This means you need him or her to come pick you up.
- Don't give up or get down on yourself if you slip—or feel like you might. This does *not* mean you are weak or have failed. Call someone in your support system to talk.

Many people in NA have a "sponsor." This is someone who has been in the program longer than they have and is someone with whom they can talk regularly and/or as needed. This person can be an invaluable source of understanding, encouragement, and support. If you are in NA, learn more about establishing a sponsor.

Prescription drug addiction can happen to anyone. But in many cases, it can be prevented. Know yourself and your family history, and be honest with all health-care providers. Don't try any drug for nonmedical purposes, even once. Most of all, remember that addictive prescription drugs are no safer or better than even the hardest street drugs. This is a truth that recovering OxyContin addict Paul Michaud, 18, can back up today. He started with the pills, but, as he told *USA Today* (June 13, 2006), he eventually became a heroin user. "I sniffed it and a week later, I was shooting," he said. "I thought I wasn't like other people doing heroin. I wasn't that low. Come to figure out, it all leads to the same place."

GLOSSARY

Addiction An emotional and physical dependence on a substance.

Brand-name drug A drug whose name is, by law, not allowed to be copied and used by other companies. For example, if a company names a drug *Vicodin* and signs up with the government to have that name protected from being copied, no other company can call its drug Vicodin. In addition, when a company invents a brand-name drug, no other company is allowed to copy the recipe for the drug for a certain amount of time. Brand-name drugs are usually more expensive than generic drugs.

Chronic Describing an illness or symptom that lasts for a long time.

Detoxification Process of removing a drug or other harmful substance from a person's body; also known as *detox.*

Extended-release drug A kind of drug that lets out medicine slowly during the course of many hours.

Food and Drug Administration (FDA) An agency in the U.S. government that keeps watch on medicines, food, and makeup to make sure that these things are safe for people to use.

General practitioner A doctor who treats many different kinds of problems, rather than focusing on treating patients who all suffer from the same illness.

Generic drug A drug that contains exactly the same ingredients as a brand-name drug but does not have the famous name. A company that wants to make a generic drug can only make it once the brand-name drug's maker has been allowed to sell the brand-name drug for a certain amount of time. Generic drugs are usually cheaper than brand-name drugs.

Hormone A substance that the body produces in one place that causes an action to happen elsewhere in the body. For example, the pancreas makes the hormone insulin, which controls how much blood sugar the body uses.

Immediate-release drug   A drug that releases medicine into the body all at once when taken.

Intravenous (IV) needle   A needle that is inserted into a person's vein and slowly drips a substance (usually medicine) into his or her body.

Narcotics   Drugs that reduce pain, may change a person's behavior, and often cause sleepiness. Narcotic medicines can be very addictive when not taken properly.

Opioid   A chemical substance that helps reduce pain. Opioids work by binding to opioid receptors in the central nervous system and the gastrointestinal tract.

Physical dependence   A condition in which a person's body becomes used to a drug and cannot work (or has a hard time working) without it.

Prescription   A "permission slip" that a doctor gives a patient to allow that patient to purchase medicine at a pharmacy.

Recreational   Nonmedical use; use of a drug to get high.

Refill   An additional supply of a prescription drug that a patient can get without having to go back to his doctor for an exam. A doctor will give a patient a prescription for refills if the patient will need to take a drug over the course of many months. Once the first supply of the drug has been used, the patient can then go to the pharmacy with the refill note and get a new supply.

Synthetic   Describing a man-made drug that is made to work like a natural substance.

Terminal illness   A disease that cannot be cured and will eventually result in death.

Tolerance   A state in which a person's body becomes used to a certain amount of a drug and no longer reacts in the same way to the same amount of the drug. The user will need to take increasing amounts of the drug in order to feel the same effects that he felt when first beginning to take it.

BIBLIOGRAPHY

Alexander, J.L., et al. "Suspected opioid-related emergency medical services encounters in a rural state, 1997–2002." *Prehospital Emergency Care* 8, no.4 (October–December 2004): 427–430.

Alter, David. "Abraham Lincoln's Home for Veterans." *The Smithsonian Associates Civil War E-Mail Newsletter* 3, no. 10 (2004). Available online. URL: http://civilwarstudies.org/ newsletter.htm. Accessed August 9, 2007.

American College of Physicians. "Cancer Pain." Available online. URL: www.acponline.org/public/h_care/3-pain.htm. Accessed August 9, 2007.

American Pain Foundation. "Chronic Pain Information Page." February 1, 2007. Available online. URL: www. painfoundation.org/page.asp?file=documents/doc_024. htm. Accessed August 9, 2007.

American Pain Foundation. "Pain Facts & Figures." Available online. URL: www.painfoundation.org/print.asp?file= Newsroom/PainFacts.htm. Accessed August 9, 2007.

American Pain Foundation. "Testimony of Howard A. Heit, MD, FACP, FASAM, Congressional Briefing: The Epidemic of Pain in America." June 13, 2006. URL: www.painfoundation. org/Action/Briefing061306/HeitTestimony.pdf Accessed February 5, 2007.

"Assisted Living Facility Resident Charged in Murder." North Country Gazette, July 19, 2006. Available online. URL: http://www.northcountrygazette.org/articles/ 071906ResidentCharged.html. Accessed August 9, 2007.

Bodine, Wendy K. "Pharmacies Tighten Security to Deter Theft." *Pharmacy Times*, April 5, 2007. Available online. URL: www.pharmacytimes.com/articleNewsletter. cfm?ID=4510. Accessed August 9, 2007.

Booth, Martin. *Opium: A History.* New York: Simon and Schuster, 1996. Quoted in "A Brief History of Opium. Available online. URL: www.heroin.org/timeline/index. html Accessed February 5, 2007.

Breen, Tom. "After OxyContin scare, Appalachian addicts turn to hydrocodone." WKRN.com, June 20, 2007. URL: www.wkrn.com. Accessed July 15, 2007.

Butterfield, Fox. "Theft of Painkiller Reflects Its Popularity on the Street." *The New York Times*, July 7, 2001. Available online. URL: www.nytimes.com. Accessed: July 15, 2007.

Collins, Eric D., et al. "Anesthesia-Assisted vs. Buprenorphine- or Clonidine-Assisted Heroin Detoxification and Naltroxene Induction." *Journal of the American Medical Association (JAMA)* 294 (2005): 903–913.

Corliss, Richard. "Who's Feeling No Pain?" *Time*, March 11, 2001. Available online. URL: www.time.com/time/magazine/article/0,9171,102079,00.html. Accessed July 15, 2007.

Fakhry, Samir M. M.D., F.A.C.S.; Rutherford, Edmund J., M.D., F.A.C.S.; Sheldon George F., M.D. "Routine Postoperative Management of the Hospitalized." *ACS Surgery.* American College of Surgeons. 2005. Available online. URL: http://www.medscape.com/viewarticle/512349. Accessed August 9, 2007.

Fishman, Scott. "Pain Question & Answer: Addiction." American Pain Foundation, March 2004. Available online. URL: www.painfoundation.org/page.asp?file=QandA/Addiction.htm. Accessed August 9, 2007.

Fishman, Scott. "Pain Question & Answer: Anti-Inflammatories For Pain." American Pain Foundation, February 1, 2007. Available online. URL: www.painfoundation.org/page.asp?file=QandA/Anti-inflammatory.htm. Accessed August 9, 2007.

Fishman, Scott. "Pain Question & Answer: Side Effects of Opioids." American Pain Foundation, February 1, 2007. Available online. URL: www.painfoundation.org/page.asp?file=QandA/SideEffects.htm. Accessed August 9, 2007.

Gaul, Gilbert M., and Mary Pat Flaherty. "Internet Trafficking in Narcotics Has Surged." *Washington Post*, October 20, 2003; A01.

"Gerald Levert." Hot105 FM, Hollywood, Fla. November 2006. URL: http://hot105fm.com/features/geraldleverttribute0207.html. Accessed July 15, 2007.

Guyette, Curt. "In Vicodin's grip." *Metro Times* (Detroit). May 23, 2001. Available online. URL: www.metrotimes.com/editorial/story.asp?id=1824. Accessed February 5, 2007. Hartenstein, Meena. "Vicodin." Youth Radio, National Public Radio. Available online. URL: www.youthradio.org/health/npr_drugs.shtml. Accessed August 9, 2007.

"The Interface Between Pain and Chemical Dependency: History." Department of Pain Medicine & Palliative Care, Beth Israel Medical Center, New York. Available online. URL: www.stoppain.org/pcd/_Library/printpage.asp?REF=/pcd/content/addiction/history.asp. Accessed August 9, 2007.

Kaufman, Gil. "Courtney Love Turns Herself In On Felony Drug Charges." MTV News, October 28, 2003. URL: www.mtv.com/news/articles/1480015/20031028/love_courtney.jhtml. Accessed July 15, 2007.

Kaushik, Sandeep. "Anatomy of a drug scare." *The Boston Phoenix*, June 21–28, 2001. Available online. URL: http://bostonphoenix.com/boston/news_features/other_stories/documents/01683284.htm. Accessed July 15, 2007.

"LA Coroner: In-N-Out chief died of overdose." *Nation's Restaurant News*, February 7, 2000. Available online. URL: http://calbears.findarticles.com/p/articles/mi_m3190/is_6_34/ai_59458469. Accessed July 15, 2007.

Lambert, David. *Evaluation of the Implementation of Maine's Prescription Drug Monitoring Program.* Report by the Muskie School of Public Service, University of Southern Maine. January 2006. Available online. URL: www.maine.gov. Accessed August 9, 2007.

"Matthew Perry Quotes." BrainyQuote.com. Available online. URL: www.brainyquote.com/quotes/quotes/m/matthewper173829.html. Accessed August 9, 2007.

Meadows, Michelle. "Prescription Drug Use and Abuse." *FDA Consumer*, September–October 2001. Available online. URL: www.fda.gov/fdac/features/2001/501_drug.html. Accessed July 15, 2007.

Meier, Barry. "Narcotic Maker Guilty of Deceit Over Marketing." *The New York Times*, May 11, 2007. Available online. URL: www.nytimes.com. Accessed August 9, 2007.

Miller, Karl E. "Continuous Infusion of IV Morphine for Cancer Pain." *American Family Physician*, January 15, 2003. Available online. URL: www.aafp.org/afp/20030115/tips/13.html

Moric, Mario, et al. "The Unfulfilled Promise of Prescription Monitoring Programs: Failure of Prescription Monitoring Programs To Reduce Narcotic Abuse Levels." *Anesthesiology* 103 (2005): A1197. Abstract available online. URL: www.asaabstracts.com. Accessed: August 9, 2007.

"Morphine for Chest Pain Increases Death Risk." Duke University Medical Center News Office, May 5, 2005. URL: www.dcri.duke.edu/news/Archives/2005/2005–05–05.jsp. Accessed August 9, 2007.

MyPainKillerAddictions.com. Available online. URL: www.mypainkilleraddictions.com. Accessed August 9, 2007.

National Pharmaceutical Council. *Pain: Current Understanding of Assessment, Management, and Treatments.* December 2001. Available online. URL: www.npcnow.org/resources/PDFs/painmonograph.pdf. Accessed: July 20, 2007.

"Nicole Richie arrested for DUI." MSNBC, December 12, 2006. Available online. URL: www.msnbc.msn.com/id/16145066. Accessed August 9, 2007.

"NIDA Community Drug Alert Bulletin: Prescription Drugs." National Institute on Drug Abuse (NIDA), September 2005. Available online. URL: www.nida.nih.gov/PrescripAlert/index.html. Accessed August 9, 2007.

"NIDA InfoFacts: High School and Youth Trends." National Institute on Drug Abuse (NIDA), December 21, 2006.

Available online. URL: www.drugabuse.gov/infofacts/ hsyouthtrends.html. Accessed August 9, 2007.

"NIDA-Sponsored Survey Shows Decrease in Illicit Drug Use among Nation's Teens but Prescription Drug Abuse Remains High." *NIH News,* December 21, 2006. Available online. URL: www.nih.gov/news/pr/dec2006/nida-21.htm. Accessed August 9, 2007.

Oldenburg, Ann. "'Friends' Star's Addiction to Vicodin is Latest Painful Hollywood Vice." *USA Today,* March 8, 2001. Available online. URL: www.opiates.com/media/ vicodin-addiction-usatoday.html Accessed July 20, 2007.

"OxyContin: Questions and Answers." U.S. Food and Drug Administration (FDA), August 2, 2001. Available online. URL: www.fda.gov/cder/drug/infopage/oxycontin/ oxycontin-qa.htm. Accessed August 9, 2007.

"Pain: Hope Through Research." National Institute of Neurological Disorders and Stroke (NINDS), July 20, 2007. Available online. URL: www.ninds.nih.gov/disorders/ chronic_pain/detail_chronic_pain.htm. Accessed August 9, 2007.

Paisner, Susan R. "Pain Patients Hurt by OxyContin Hype." *The Pain Practitioner,* Summer 2002. Available online. URL: www.aapainmanage.org. Accessed July 20, 2007.

Partners Against Pain (Purdue Pharma L.P.). *Pain in America.* Available online. URL: www.partnersagainstpain.com/ index-hs.aspx?sid=24&aid=7798. Accessed August 9, 2007.

Payne, January W. "A Dangerous Mix: Some Drugs Don't Go Together; Web Sites May Help Flag Them." *Washington Post*, February 27, 2007: F.1

Phillips, Lauren, and Tina Reed. "Unhealthy dosage." *The State News*, March 14, 2005. Available online. URL: www. statenews.com. Accessed July 15, 2007.

"Police Arrest 7 In Forged Prescription Drug Ring." News4Jax. com, September 14, 2006. Available online. URL: www. news4jax.com/news/9851061/detail.html Accessed July 15, 2007.

"Police Log." Web site of the town of Boone, N.C. March 16, 2007. Available online. URL: www.townofboone.net/departments/police/stats/news.html. Accessed August 9, 2007.

Rasor, Joseph, and Gerald Harris. "Opioid Use for Moderate to Severe Pain." *The Journal of the American Osteopathic Association* 105:6 (June 2005): 2–7.

Reckitt Benckiser Pharmaceuticals, Inc. "History of Opioids." Available online. URL: www.suboxone.com/patients/opioiddependence/history.aspx. Accessed August 9, 2007.

Rosenberg, Tina. "Doctor or Drug Pusher?" *The New York Times*, June 17, 2007. Available online. URL: www.nytimes.com. Accessed August 9, 2007.

"RX Monitoring Programs Ineffective in Curbing Drug Abuse." Alliance of State Pain Initiatives, May 2006. Available online. URL: http://aspi.wisc.edu/newsletter/0605.html. Accessed August 9, 2007.

"Safety Concerns Associated with Over-the-Counter Drug Products Containing Analgesic/Antipyretic Active Ingredients for Internal Use." U.S. Food and Drug Administration (FDA), January 22, 2004. Available online. URL: www.fda.gov/cder/drug/analgesics/SciencePaper.htm. Accessed August 9, 2007.

Satel, Sally. "OxyContin Half-Truths Can Cause Suffering." *USA Today*, October 27, 2003. Available online. URL: www.usatoday.com. Accessed July 20, 2007.

Self, Wes. "A Brief History of the Opioids." Davidson College, Fall 1999. Available online. URL: www.bio.davidson.edu/courses/anphys/1999/Self/History.htm. Accessed August 9, 2007.

Silverman, Steven M. "Jack Osbourne Admits to Oxy Addiction." *People Magazine* online, July 3, 2003. Available online. URL: www.people.com/people/article/0,26334,626374,00.html. Accessed August 9, 2007.

Teens and Prescription Drugs. Report by the Office of National Drug Control Policy, Executive Office of the President.

February 2007. Available online. URL: www.mediacampaign. org/teens/brochure.pdf. Accessed July 20, 2007.

Texas Commission on Alcohol and Drug Abuse. "Abuse of Codeine Cough Syrup a Growing Problem." October 14, 1999. Available online. URL: www.jointogether.org/news/ research/pressreleases/1999/abuse-of-codeine-cough-syrup. html. Accessed July 20, 2007.

"Thanks to Online Pharmacies, Addiction Can Be Just a Click Away." Narconon Southern California. Available online. URL: www.drugrehabamerica.net/user-news.htm?id=64. Accessed August 9, 2007.

Thomas, Evan. "I Am Addicted to Prescription Pain Medication." *Newsweek*, October 20, 2003.Available online. URL: www.msnbc.msn.com/id/3158206/. Accessed August 9, 2007.

"Trauma Pain." iVillage Total Health. Available online. URL: http://pain.health.ivillage.com/common/articleprintfriendly. cfm?artid=1825. Accessed August 9, 2007.

Trigaux, Robert. "Strong dose of hype for OxyContin inexcusable." *St. Petersburg Times*, November 10, 2003. Available online. URL: www.sptimes.com/2003/11/10/Columns/ Strong_dose_of_hype_f.shtml. Accessed July 20, 2007.

University of Chicago Medical Center. "As morphine turns 200, drug that blocks its side effects reveals new secrets." May 19, 2005. Available online. URL: www.uchospitals. edu/news/2005/20050519-morphine.html. Accessed August 9, 2007.

University of Maryland Medical Center. "Back pain and sciatica." Available online. URL: www.umm.edu /patiented/ articles/what_low_back_pain_sciatica_000054_1.htm. Accessed August 9, 2007.

U.S. Department of Health and Human Services, Substance Abuse and Mental Health Services Administration (SAMHSA). "Federal Report Shows New Nonmedical Users of Prescription Pain Relievers Outnumbered New Marijuana

Users Between 2002 and 2004." October 27, 2006. Available online. URL: www.samhsa.gov/news/newsreleases/061027_PainRelievers.htm. Accessed August 9, 2007.

U.S. Drug Enforcement Administration. "Drug Scheduling." Available online. URL: www.usdoj.gov/dea/pubs/scheduling.html. Accessed August 9, 2007.

U.S. Drug Enforcement Administration. "Narcotics." Chap. 4 in *Drugs of Abuse*. 2005. Available online. URL: www.usdoj.gov/dea/pubs/abuse/4-narc.htm. Accessed July 20, 2007.

U.S. Drug Enforcement Administration. "Fentanyl." Available online. URL: www.usdoj.gov/dea/concern/fentanyl.html. Accessed August 9, 2007.

U.S. Drug Enforcement Administration, Office of Diversion Control. "A Closer Look at State Prescription Monitoring Programs." Available online. URL: www.deadiversion.usdoj.gov/faq/rx_monitor.htm. Accessed August 9, 2007.

U.S. Drug Enforcement Administration, Office of Diversion Control. "Drugs and Chemicals of Concern: Hydromorphone." Available online. URL: www.deadiversion.usdoj.gov/drugs_concern/hydromorphone.htm. Accessed August 9, 2007.

"Vicodin." Recovery Connection. Available online. URL: www.recoveryconnection.org/drug_index/vicodin.php. Accessed August 9, 2007.

"Vicodin: Overdosages & Contraindications." Available online. URL: www.rxlist.com/cgi/generic/hydrocod_od.htm. Accessed August 9, 2007.

Weissman, David E. "Fast Fact and Concept #071: Meperidine for Pain: What Is All the Fuss?" American Academy of Hospice and Palliative Medicine, June 2002. Available online. URL: www.aahpm.org/cgi-bin/wkcgi/view?status=A%20&search=15. Accessed August 2007.

"What is the Role of Aspirin?" National Reye's Syndrome Foundation, 2005. Available online. URL: www.reyessyndrome.org/aspirin.htm. Accessed August 9, 2007.

Bibliography

Zuckerbrod, Nancy. "GAO: OxyContin Claims Unsubstanti-
ated." *The Oklahoman*, January 23, 2004. Available online.
URL: www.mapinc.org/drugnews/v04/n154/a04.html?1496.
Accessed August 9, 2007.

FURTHER READING

Durham, Michael. *Painkillers and Tranquilizers. Just the Facts.* Chicago: Heinemann, 2003.

Fitzhugh, Karla. *Prescription Drug Abuse. What's the Deal?* Chicago: Heinemann, 2005.

Olive, M. Foster. *Prescription Pain Relievers.* Philadelphia: Chelsea House Publishers, 2005.

Pinsky, Drew. *When Painkillers Become Dangerous: What Everyone Needs to Know About OxyContin and Other Prescription Drugs.* Center City, Minn.: Hazelden, 2004.

Youngs, Bettie B. *A Teen's Guide to Living Drug Free.* Deerfield Beach, Fla.: HCI Teens, 2003.

WEB SITES

NIDA FOR TEENS: THE SCIENCE BEHIND DRUG ABUSE

http://teens.drugabuse.gov

On this site, teens can learn about prescription medications, read about other teens' real-life experiences with drugs, and participate in interactive games and quizzes.

JUST THINK TWICE

http://www.justthinktwice.com

This interactive Web site, which is run by the U.S. Drug Enforcement Agency (DEA), provides teens with information about drugs of abuse.

TEENS HEALTH

http://www.teenshealth.org

Sponsored by the Nemours Foundation, this site offers information on health topics that are important to young people. Advice for getting help with drugs is included.

PHOTO CREDITS

INDEX

medicinal use of, 58–61
trends in abuse of, 22
OxyContin and, PMPs and, 84

P

pain, 12–16, 25–26. *See also* chronic
  pain
Paisner, Susan R., 59
Palladone, 71
palliative care, 63–64
Paracelsus, 20
patches, 33, 70, 71
patient-controlled analgesia (PCA),
  28, 64
Percocet, 68, 76, 77
Percodan, 68
Perry, Matthew, 36, 38
pharmaceutical companies, 73. *See
  also* specific companies
physical dependence, 20, 78–79
physical therapy, 26
poppies, 17, 66
prescription fraud, 82–83
Prescription Monitoring Programs
  (PMPs), 81–84
prostaglandins, NSAIDS and, 14
Purdue Frederick, 57
Purdue Pharma, 49–50, 52, 56–58

R

rapid detox, 89–91
Reye's Syndrome, 14
Richie, Nicole, 38
robbery, 52–53
Robiquet, Pierre-Jean, 66
Rosenberg, Tina, 60–61

S

salicylate, 14
schedules, 41
Schofield, Regina B., 84
Serturner, Friedrich Wilhelm, 20–21,
  62–63, 66
skin, 33, 70, 71
sleeping pills, 46
snorting, OxyContin and, 51
Snyder, H. Guy, 44
soldiers' disease, 65
spinal cord injuries, 29–30
sponsors, 95

Stallard, Robert, 55
Substance Abuse Treatment Facility
  Locator, 88
Sumeria, 19
surgery, 24–29, 68
Sydenham, Thomas, 20
synthetic drugs, 18, 66, 67–71, 93
syringes, 65

T

teenagers, 40–41, 74
TeensHealth.com, 94–95
terminal illnesses, 63–64
thebaine, 67
theft, 52–53
Thomas, Jim, 52
Thornburg, John, 75
tolerance, 20, 71, 78–79
traumatic injuries, opioids and, 29–30
Tritter, Michael, 46–47
Twillman, Robert, 84
Tylenol, 16

U

Udell, Howard R., 57
ultra-rapid detox, 90–91

V

Valium, 73
vaults, 52–53
Veterans Affairs Medical Center
  (Boston), 55
Vicodin
  abuse of, 40–44
  celebrity abuse of, 38–39
  dangers of, 44–48
  medicinal use of, 37–38
  side effects of, 44–46
  trends in abuse of, 22

W

Web sites, 43
Williams, Danielle, 55–56
withdrawal, 79, 89, 93
Wood, Alexander, 65
Wright, C.R., 21

X

Xanax, 77

ABOUT THE AUTHORS

AMY E. BREGUET is freelance writer whose focus is on educational topics. She has written about health, safety, and related subjects in a variety of formats, many geared toward young people. She lives in Southampton, Massachusetts, with her husband and two young children.

Series introduction author **RONALD J. BROGAN** is the Bureau Chief for the New York City office of D.A.R.E. (Drug Abuse Resistance Education) America, where he trains and coordinates more than 100 New York City police officers in program-related activities. He also serves as a D.A.R.E. regional director for Oregon, Connecticut, Massachusetts, Maine, New Hampshire, New York, Rhode Island, and Vermont. In 1997, Brogan retired from the U.S. Drug Enforcement Administration (DEA), where he served as a special agent for 26 years. He holds bachelor's and master's degrees in criminal justice from the City University of New York.